Temptation

Help for Struggling Christians

Charles
Durham

InterVarsity Press
Downers Grove
Illinois 60515

InterVarsity Press is the book-publishing division of Inter-Varsity Christian Fellowship, a student movement active on campus at hundreds of universities, colleges and schools of nursing. For information about local and regional activities, write IVCF, 233 Langdon St., Madison, WI 53703.

Distributed in Canada through InterVarsity Press, 1875 Leslie St., Unit 10, Don Mills, Ontario M3B 2M5, Canada.

Cover illustration: Marcus Hamilton

All Scripture quotations, unless otherwise indicated, are from the Revised Standard Version of the Bible, copyrighted 1946, 1952 © 1971, 1973.

The quotation on pp. 138-39 is taken from Mere Christianity by C. S. Lewis. Copyright 1943, 1945, 1952 by Macmillan Publishing Co., Inc. Used by permission of Macmillan Publishing Co., New York, and Fontana Paperbacks, London.

ISBN 0-87784-382-1

Printed in the United States of America

Library of Congress Cataloging in Publication Data

Durham, Charles, 1939-
    Temptation, help for struggling Christians.

    Includes bibliographical references.
    1. Temptation.   I. Title.
BT725.D87   248.8'6   82-153
ISBN 0-87784-382-1   AACR2

17 16 15 14 13 12 11 10 9 8 7 6 5 4 3 2
96 95 94 93 92 91 90 89 88 87 86 85 84 83

*With deep affection, this book
is dedicated to my parents,
Joe and Marian Durham*

Acknowledgments

I want to express my sincere thanks to those who helped in the formation of this book. Clifford Arndt, my close friend for many years, first encouraged me to write for publication. Duane and Marilyn Ramsey and Ed and Deva Cupp read the manuscript and strengthened me with their enthusiasm. Elaine Vaughan and Clark Harbach gave me helpful advice. Larry and Fran Greathouse will never know how much their constant optimism meant to me. Wilford and Louise Crist gave me the continual support of their prayers. The people of my congregation, Prairie View Church of the Brethren, freely allowed me the time necessary to do the work. I especially want to thank my wife Linda for listening to my endless rehearsal of the ideas contained in Temptation *and for her constructive suggestions. And last of all, I want to thank my children, Mark, David, Deborah and Rebekah, whose interest and joy added to my desire to write.*

Introduction

"What do *you* do when you're tempted?" The question was directed to no one in particular, but an overweight young woman answered laughing, "When I meet temptation, I eat it!" The group joined in laughter. Then a serious young fellow of about thirty said without a smile, "What do I do when I'm tempted? I'll tell you what I do. I yield!" Again the others laughed, this time with surprise. But I knew that the young man had not intended to be funny; he was hurting, and he was groping for the answer to his personal failure.

I wondered about the group members: why did they

laugh? Could it have been out of emotional relief, each one secretly saying, "Thank God! I'm not alone!"

This book has been written because so many of us, when we meet temptation, do just as the young man did: we yield. And of course that produces pain and disappointment, along with the realization that we have fallen short of God's desire.

Another reason for this book is that temptation is a greater problem these days than it used to be. There is more of it around, and it is more intense and more complex. This generation is forced to meet more temptation head-on than perhaps any other.

How do I win the battle against temptation? This is the question I will try to answer, I will not offer ten easy steps to overcoming because no such steps exist. I have tried to avoid giving easy answers. We are frequently offered a short-cut or a "key" that will make it all easy. As a result, we are left with unbalanced ideas of what the battle is about and how it is to be fought. The subject is many-sided, so I have taken an analytical approach and tried to leave out nothing that is basic. This is why many chapters deal simply with the basics of Christian discipleship. These general matters are part of the battle against the specific problem of temptation. Rather than offering some "key to victory," I have tried to go to the base line and have pointed out what we must do if we are to fight this battle in a biblical way.

My qualifications for writing on this subject may be illustrated by telling you about a friend of mine who is a successful teacher of grade-school math. In a conversation with a principal, she confessed that as a child she had a terrible time with arithmetic of any kind. Yet, there she was, teaching math and doing very well in helping the students understand it. How could that be? The principal was not surprised. He said that he had found that those teachers who have had a hard time with a subject as a child have had to study more carefully and as a result are better able to teach that subject to others. Not only do they know the material in greater detail, but they also understand the problems that the slower students face.

I think I have had to work more carefully than most in order to understand and live as a Christian. My hope is that as a result, I may understand more clearly the problems of those who struggle with the Christian life.

This book has twin premises. One is that salvation is by the grace of God alone, a free gift through the substitutionary death of Christ—plus nothing. The other is that the process by which we become more Christlike is *not* substitutionary, but requires work on our part. This means that the book is written for Christians only. It does not describe how an unregenerate person can be reformed. Rather, it describes how an already converted person—especially one who admits to weaknesses and struggles to make headway up the ladder of victory without much success—can live a more Christlike life.

No matter how weak you may be, if you read carefully, I believe you will find a rung on the ladder low enough to reach. Then, by God's grace you will be able to begin climbing.

If you want to remember what is written here, and if you want these pages to work for you, make up a set of notes. Write chapter summaries or your personal notations that contain what is most helpful to you. Slip them into a folder or pin them on your bulletin board, and review them periodically. Every time you review your notes, the material will go to work in your mind and eventually will become a permanent, working part of your life.

May this book be an instructive tool in the Spirit's hands and an encouragement to those who want not to yield, but to win.

Part One

Sources of the
Problem

1

The External Problem: The World and the Devil

"Now, in so far as you approach
temptation to a man, you do him
injury: and if he is overcome, you
share his guilt."
Samuel Johnson

"The god of this world has blinded
[their] minds."
Paul (2 Cor 4:4)

ON A MOONLESS, STORMY NIGHT two hundred years ago, four men stood on a grassy knoll overlooking the North Atlantic and peered seaward at a ship's light glowing in the blackness. One man paced back and forth, leading a horse with a lighted lantern tied to its nodding chin. Soon, a short distance at sea, the ship would go aground and be wrecked by pounding water. Eventually the sands would hide the wreck, but not before every last thing of value had been taken by these men—who made their living as wreckers.

The story is true. Near what is now called Cape Hatteras in North Carolina is an island of sand that runs up and down the coast, forming a kind of protective barrier against the seas. These island dunes reach out, just beneath the waves, making an underwater shelf called Diamond Shoals, the graveyard of the Atlantic. There the rotting remains of at least twenty-three hundred ships lie trapped in the sand. Many of those ships foundered by accident, but the fate of others was a result of treachery.

With a lighted lantern fastened to the head of an old nag of a horse, these men of Nag's Head—that was the name of their village—went out on stormy nights to draw ships onto Diamond Shoals. On a promontory overlooking the ocean, the horse was led back and forth, up and down. And often, on the seaward side of Diamond Shoals, a ship's pilot, standing at the helm searching for a passage up the coast, would see the bobbing light and take it for the stern light of a ship that had found safe passage. The helmsman would spin the wheel and follow. Within minutes the ship was aground on the shoals. If there was time the crew took to the lifeboats. If there was not time, it was all the same to the wreckers.

Next morning the wreckers came out in dories to inspect their latest prize. With luck there would be ship's timber for houses, new utensils and dishes, perhaps even silver-plate for their homes and money for their purses. It was a profitable business. Even now visitors to Nag's Head will see old houses built and furnished with plunder taken by the wreckers so long ago.

In this opening chapter we look at spiritual wreckers— the world and the devil. "World" does not mean simply the people who inhabit the earth. It means, rather, the system of thought and the lifestyle that stands in opposition to God. The "wreckers" of this chapter are those men and women of the world who follow those opposing patterns and styles and then militantly work to draw others after them.

The World

I am convinced that there is more temptation in our day than ever before. It is increasing in several ways. First, it is increasing in sheer amount. There are no new temptations, but the old ones come along more often. There are no new desires, no new mental, physical or spiritual equipment with previously unknown longings to be satisfied. Our technology, however, provides us with tools which whet the old appetites to new sharpness and bring the old temptations into the reach of every person. Western culture is a Vanity Fair that bombards us with opportunities for greed, over-consumption, dishonesty, sexual misbehavior, excessive leisure and disregard for others. We are constantly being reminded of our appetites and of opportunities to satisfy them in ways that are illegitimate or excessive.

Second, to yield to temptation is increasingly accepted. The lines of right and wrong have been redrawn by public opinion. Many behaviors once forbidden are now perfectly acceptable to society. In some cases this is good, but in others the wrong choice has been made.

Third, temptation has increased in intensity. The appeals to greed are brighter and slicker, more lifelike and real, abundantly capable of exciting the imagination to previously unknown levels. In fact, modern advertising is so brilliant that it does our imagining for us!

Fourth, temptation has increased in pervasiveness. Unless one becomes a recluse, it is no longer possible to build walls high enough to keep its appeal away. It is more pervasive among the very young. Grade schoolers are hit with drug traffic, and, according to Dr. C. Everett Koop, with sex education that is pornographic. Koop has said that youngsters "with peach fuzz on their cheeks are made to believe that if they are not sexually active by the time they are fourteen, life has passed them by and left them in a very dry place."[1] Even three-year-olds are urged via television to become overconsumers (a euphemism for "greedy").

Fifth, temptation has increased in persuasiveness. We are told that there are good reasons, based on science, psychology and sociology, for forgetting the old rules of behavior. This places us in a very different ball game. It is no longer a matter of everyone being in agreement about what is wrong and what is right, with some folk conforming and some not. There is no longer any agreement!

For example, in the 1920s, if you had tapped a flapper and her date on the shoulder and said, "What you are doing is morally wrong," she might have smiled coyly and said, "Yeah, we know. But it's fun!" If you were to accost today's free-spirited couple in the same way, the answer would more likely be, "Who's to say it's wrong?" Who indeed? For many in our time agree with B. F. Skinner who has called God the "archetypal pattern of an explanatory fiction."[2] Given that view of God and life, all answers to questions of right and wrong elude us, and we are free to do what we wish. Not only are we free, but we seem to have good reasons for espousing the sexual revolution, the drug revolution and all kinds of other self-serving behaviors.

Immoral Pressures

So much for temptation's arising from progressive changes in values. Now consider the sheer force of direct appeal to do things we continue to believe are wrong.

We may agree that we should not be self-centered. But everywhere, by billboards, TV and radio commercials, magazine ads and newspapers, we are encouraged to be selfish. Madison Avenue appeals to our impatience, pride, selfishness, laziness and pure greed. In the end, through constant exposure, we unconsciously change our beliefs about right and wrong.

Next, think of the pressures of advertising and media on sexual desire. Sexuality is wholly a good thing, one of

God's best gifts. But in today's world sex is just another pitch to sell products. Toothpaste, movie tickets, clothing, cars, almost anything you might name is sold by sexual suggestion. As a result, our environment is filled with such appeals to a degree not known in the past. These stimuli surface in popular music. *Newsweek* reported that in one of Donna Summer's most popular songs, she vocally simulates twenty-two sexual orgasms.[3]

Visual advertising uses the same forwardness. One large poster advertising jeans shows the backside of a tightly jeaned model. It is captioned with the teasing invitation "feel the fit." And what woman is not at least vaguely aware that she has a certain sexual advantage if it "looks like she's not wearin' nothin' "?

I am not saying that our society should return to floor-length dresses and wrist-length sleeves. In fact, properly balanced, some new liberties are a moral improvement on the old restrictions. But they are not properly balanced in our society. It is the imbalance created by the abuse of sexuality to sell that alarms me and damages our moral sensibilities.

Think, too, of the inroads temptation has made on our social institutions, especially the family. Throughout the Western world the divorce rate is extremely high in comparison to the first quarter of this century and before. In a new way men and women have squared off against each other in a battle for power and position. Children are suffering enormously, and the shelter of even the Christian home is being badly eroded.

Mental Pressures
Murray Banks has said that of any twenty-five children in any playground, "two will be in an institution for the insane before their lives are over; two will be profoundly neurotic; two more will be deeply neurotic; four more will be mildly

neurotic, and eight to ten will be fairly normal."[4] If that assessment is accurate, then only thirty-two to forty per cent of us are "fairly normal," and sixty to sixty-eight per cent are unbalanced to some degree.

What has this to do with temptation? As a general rule, the less mental and emotional balance we have, the more numerous and severe our temptations and the poorer our ability to cope with them. Increased mental instability is one more of the many reasons which indicate to me that temptation is a greater and more difficult problem to deal with than in the past.

Diabolical Events

April 1945. In an underground bunker, Hitler and the Chancellery of the Third Reich faced their final days. Hitler dictated his Political Testament. Then, on the 29th, word reached him of Mussolini's execution in Italy two days before. The Russians occupied most of Berlin, leaving no hope of survival.

On the morning of the 29th, Hitler married his mistress, Eva Braun. Later that day, he arranged for his beloved dogs to be put to death, and otherwise made preparation for the end. About 2:00 o'clock the next afternoon he ate his last lunch and with his new bride entered their apartment. With the Russians scarcely a block away, they killed themselves, the Fuehrer with a pistol, Eva with poison.

According to Hitler's own instructions, the bodies were carried to the gardens, placed in a crater made by a Russian shell, drenched in gasoline, and set ablaze. It was a "Viking funeral," leaving nothing of the bodies for desecration— not a bit of bone nor an identifiable ash.

Would God that the results of his life could be wiped out as easily and completely as his bones! Germany was ruined. Robust health and joy had been shattered. Fortunes had disappeared. Millions were killed. A large part of the European Jewish community had been exterminated. Things as they had been could never be called back.

That these events transpired is a horror beyond the ability of language to convey. And the years since Hitler have witnessed atrocities and genocides elsewhere just as horrifying. Some say the twentieth century is the bloodiest in history. This is a bitter puzzle. Every mind that has ever wakened to the hard facts of life asks, "How can it be? What is the source of evil in the world?"

The word *demonic* has been used to describe Hitler, Idi Amin, Pol Pot and others. Perhaps most historians use the word figuratively, but they come closer to the truth than they dream. When in any context we use the word *diabolic* to explain the evil, discord, pain, death and the temptations leading to them, we express something profoundly true.

I do not want to leave the impression with the reader that every evil or unpleasant event has Satan standing directly behind it as the cause. But it is safe to say that had it not been for his original intrusion, evil and unpleasant events would not occur.

Dark Earth Invader

The Scriptures lift the veil only very slightly from the origin of evil. It was born not in a process, but in an individual. Both the Old and New Testaments speak of a person who is the Adversary (Job 1—2; Zech 3:1-2; Mt 4:10; 1 Thess 2:18). In the New Testament we are told of the same person, using other names: the Destroyer (Rev 9:11), "the accuser of our brethren" (Rev 12:10), "the deceiver of the whole world" (Rev 12:9), "the evil one" (Mt 13:18, 38), and "the god of this world" (2 Cor 4:4). In both Matthew 4:3 and 1 Thessalonians 3:5, he is called "the tempter."

Thus, the devil is the second of the two great external sources of temptation. Any discussion of overcoming must take him into account. Even our secular literature reveals that when we think deeply about temptation, we think about this dark enemy of God. For example, there is Goethe's Mephistopheles, J. R. R. Tolkein's Dark Lord, C. S. Lewis's Bent Oyarsa, and perhaps even *Star Wars'* Darth Vader (Dar'th 'Vader = Dark Earth Invader?). These imaginative types are nearer the heart of things than the modern "fantasies" that exclude them.

A clinical psychologist talking with a Christian brain surgeon once said, "I don't understand how people can get their lives into such messes!" The surgeon responded, "You forget about the devil!"

I leave such questions as, Why does God allow the devil to exist and to act as he does? Who is the devil? Why does he tempt people? to a later chapter. For now, just remember the brain surgeon's comment. Until you take your real enemy into account, you will be fighting your battle in only half-light; and that is a clear disadvantage.

Several years ago the Israeli Government Tourist Office advertised trips to Israel in the *National Geographic*. The full-page ad showed a smiling man sitting in a relaxed position with his legs crossed and a tea cup in hand, floating on the Dead Sea. The ad said, "cups and saucers float on it . . . And so do you . . . You can float clear to Sodom, if you like."[5]

The application hardly needs to be made. Christians can do exactly that in the present atmosphere. The current running so strongly against us, and the devil's treachery, make resistance very difficult indeed. Each of us is faced with a personal choice to wage war or to lie back comfortably and float to Sodom.

Summary
There are merchandizers around in great numbers who are happy to make their living by wrecking the values of others. Because of such people, the problem of temptation

from the external world is growing. It is growing in sheer amount, in social acceptance, in "quality," in pervasiveness, and in its power to persuade.

To wage war against temptation successfully implies living biblical lives, and this in turn implies understanding the biblical teachings on the subject.

There are two sources of temptation which are completely external to the Christian, but which she or he must take into account: the world and the devil. In profound ways, the wreckage that we see about us is the work of this earth invader. He is your enemy and mine, a real part of the problem.

2

The Internal Problem: The Flesh

"Temptations imply desires within;
men ought not to say, 'How
powerfully the devil tempts,' but 'How
strongly I am tempted.' "
H. W. Beecher

"Each person is tempted when he is
lured and enticed by his own desire."
James (1:14)

"HOW CONVENIENT! SOMEONE violates the rules of human order and decency, blames it on other people, then invents a 'devil' to take what's left of the blame, and goes off scot-free."

It does sound that way, doesn't it? We tend to blame anyone but ourselves for our sin. One of the great dangers of the Christian life is that with the world and the devil to blame, we will refuse to shoulder our own part of the responsibility. Psychologists call it "projection." They mean that we project blame away from ourselves.

Now, the world *does* bear blame. Temptation *has* multiplied in our time. And the Bible tells us that the devil is real, a force to be reckoned with. That much is not projection. But when the Christian begins to think, "the devil made me do it," that is projection.

What I Am

We must admit that we have personal responsibility in the matter of temptation. Let's face it. If the world and the devil did not have something that we want, they would have no power over us at all. There would be no temptation.

Christians often say, "I don't want to do that, but I find myself doing it anyway." Paul says the very same thing in Romans, but a more complete statement would be, "I want *not* to do that, and at the same time I want to do it." Fact: we humans often want contradictory things at the same moment.

At one time I may both hate a specific act and also love it. If I go ahead and do the thing, then I demonstrate that at least for that moment, I loved it more than I hated it. We are not lured by that which we do not desire in one way or another. If the *ex*ternal has no appeal to the *in*ternal, there is no temptation. The items so attractively displayed by the world and the devil lure me only because I am a human being who sometimes wants what Satan and the world have to offer.

Out of the Depths

When we ask, What am I? we must admit to not knowing the full answer. Just as we do not know about all the creatures that live in the ocean depths, we do not fully know our own hearts. This article appeared in the *Mystic Press* (the newspaper published in West Mystic, Connecticut) on July 31, 1874:

Schooner PEARL, 150 tons, James Floyd, master, with a crew of six, was reported sunk by a giant squid in Lat.

8.50 N., Long. 84.05 E. on May 10th, 1874. The sinking was witnessed and reported by passenger steamer STRATHOWEN bound from Columbo to Madras. Passengers first noted a large brownish mass lying on the surface between the steamer and the schooner, which was becalmed two or three miles away. Someone on the schooner fired a rifle at the object and it began to move toward the schooner and squeezed on board between the fore and mainmast, pulling the vessel over and sinking it.[1]

You may doubt the accuracy of that account and say that such creatures do not exist, and you may be right. But then again, you may be wrong. This is an excellent picture of our situation. Who knows what impulses and desires lie fathoms down in the human heart? This is one point at which there is at least a modicum of agreement between the Bible and Sigmund Freud. Freud believed that the greater portion of mental attitudes, views, hopes, fears and general workings of the mind were unknown to the individual. He believed that beneath our conscious thought is a mass of primordial drives and wishes.

Through the prophet Jeremiah, God tells us something very much like that. He declared, "The heart is deceitful . . . and desperately wicked: who can know it?" (Jer 17:9 KJV). Who among us has never been stunned with surprise to find that we were entertaining a wish of which we had thought ourselves incapable? Desires are like monsters from the deep and are perfectly capable of coming to the surface in an unguarded moment, responding to an unusual provocation.

Rising to the Bait
James tells us how temptation occurs: "Each person is tempted when he is lured and enticed by his own desire" (Jas 1:14). The Greek word translated "enticed" is related

to the word *bait*. James, using a metaphor drawn from fishing, said that being tempted is a matter of being lured.

Imagine Satan going fishing. He is trolling his lure in the waters of the mind. The Christian's desire is enticed like a fish to strike at the lure. When the hook is set, the desire is "taken in tow,"[2] and pulled from the water.

Of course the important question is, What is the lure that he uses? James answers that Satan uses anything that will correspond to the person's desire; in other words, anything for which he or she has a taste.

Desire is a morally neutral word that implies neither good nor evil. This is shown by the fact that the same Greek word used by James occurs in an entirely positive context: "I have earnestly desired to eat this passover with you before I suffer" (Lk 22:15). (*Lust* in KJV is simply an attempt to give a negative translation to a negative context—James 1:14—but the Greek word is the same in both texts.) Here is the point: James tells us not that Satan lures us by appealing to our *bad* desires, but by appealing to our legitimate desires with *ill*egitimate opportunities.

Desires in themselves are not wrong. In fact, they are God's creation. Granted, they can be twisted into very ugly shapes, but in their original form they are wholly good. G. Campbell Morgan said, "If you can only get far enough back into the mystery of your sin you will find a desire which is not wrong in itself."[3] It is when desire fastens to an object outside the will of God that sin is conceived.

For example, let us say that there is a little house out in the country. It is surrounded by tall, green trees and a wide carpet of lawn. The setting is peaceful and very beautiful. The little home appeals to you and you decide that you want it. Is your desire wrong? No. The longings for peace and beauty are created by God and given to you as a good gift.

But then you visit the owner. "Is it for sale?" "Yes." "How

much?" But the price is too high. You cannot afford it. Then, from somewhere in the deep waters of your mind comes a thought—a lure trailing by—and your perfectly legitimate desire rises to the bait. "You can have that money," it says. "Alter the books. You're clever enough, and no one will ever know." The direction the story takes from this point depends entirely on your personal submission to God and how accustomed you are to disciplining your desires.

Back of every theft there was somewhere a desire for ownership that became misdirected. Behind every act of gluttony there was once a pleasure in good food that God gave. Beneath every instance of adultery has been a desire to be loved, to experience closeness, to know the warmth of human touch and to have satisfied a sexual drive that was conceived in God's mind. Even behind an act of violence is somewhere a good desire that has been frustrated and unmet until twisted into criminal form. This does not justify any sin; it merely shows more clearly what temptation really is.

Temptation, then, means being lured to fulfill good desires in some illegitimate way. The crime of transgression is compounded by the fact that God has given us a framework in which to satisfy our desires legitimately, freely and joyfully.

Summary
The Christians are in danger of blaming the world and the devil for their own failings. They will take a substantial step forward by confessing that they are victims of their own failure to discipline the desires which God has given them. If they find themselves unable to apply the basic biblical disciplines, they must set out to learn those disciplines and then put them to work in their own lives.

3

What Causes Weakness?

"I see the devil's hook, and yet
cannot help nibbling at his bait."
Moses Adams

"The spirit indeed is willing, but
the flesh is weak."
Jesus (Mt 26:41)

HAVE YOU EVER PRAYED A prayer like this one? "Lord, I've
brought this problem to you before. I've lain face down on
the ground in the night and poured out my heart until
there was nothing left to pour. I've wept until there were no
more tears. I've prayed until I was certain that my besetting
sin would never bother me again. 'This time,' I thought, 'by
God's grace I will win!' Faith welled up inside. 'At last I've
got it!' But, Lord, it came back. Just a little at a time, until
it filled my thoughts from morning until night. Finally, I
just gave in. Lord, why am I so weak?"

A preacher was once asked to speak at a rescue mission in

the skid-row district of a large city. He rose and began to recite Rudyard Kipling's "If," a poem which says that if we are able to do certain things—keep our heads, trust ourselves, wait, be hated without hating, dream, think, keep our virtue, hold on, fill every minute with "sixty seconds worth of distance run"—then "Yours is the Earth and everything that's in it, And—which is more—you'll be a Man, my son!" As the preacher completed the oration a down-and-out looking man stood to his feet and called out, "Yeah preacher, but what if you can't?" That derelict's question is the question of this book: Why am I unable to do what is right, and what do I do about it?

Surveying the Problem

There is a romantic idea that if in life we do our best, God's grace will make up the difference and keep us out of trouble. That just is not true. Our mistakes, our sins, our misconceptions will eventually work their way into our personality, despite the best intentions. Good will and fine purpose will not prevent our suffering the consequences of not having known how to build the right kind of character. To win the battle against temptation we must know what we need to do and how to do it, and then we must put that knowledge into action. God's grace and personal competency (not merely good intentions) are both necessary.

Take mountaineers for example. They do not climb haphazardly. They know mountains to be notoriously unforgiving things. So months ahead of time they sit down to ask questions and lay plans. Huge topographical maps cover the walls. Those who have already made the climb sit down with them and tell all that they have learned. Before a foot is set on the trail, the climbers know which approaches to take, how rugged the climb will be, the possible weather conditions, and every other bit of information they can possibly glean. The physical conditioning and development of skills necessary to overcome the mountain's challenges are not gained overnight; they are the fruit of years of exercise, training and practice at less challenging climbs.

Setting out to become more like Jesus Christ, Christians need to do something very much like that. This is part of what Jesus meant when he told us to "count the cost" (Lk 14:28). So, let's ask, What are the reasons for our weaknesses? and What must we do to overcome those weaknesses?

The Causes of Human Weakness

moral

There are several basic reasons for the human condition of moral weakness. First, our spiritual nature is fallen. With the fall, humanity was broken in every respect: will, loyalties, loves, and the singleness of devotion to God were all miserably damaged. The human being thereafter was characterized by a double will and a double behavior pattern, a condition that exists yet today in all believers. In short, when our first parents fell in the garden, our spiritual nature fell with them. Because our affections were divided at that moment, the strength of resolution to serve God fled from all succeeding generations.

Second, we are weak because of our physical natures. Human beings are not pure spirit, but spiritual-physical beings functioning in a material world. On this physical plane, also, the fall did its damage. Your body places limitations on you, colors your outlook and affects your decisions, even decisions that have a bearing on your relationship to God. Biology impinges on theology. Your body influences your behavior through its genetics, the chemistry of its glandular functions, enough or too little sleep, stress, and many other ways.

Think, for example, of the disciples sleeping when they should have been praying. Jesus said, "the spirit indeed is willing, but the flesh is weak" (Mk 14:38). These men should have been praying, but their physical bodies demanded rest. If we go for a substantial period of time without sleep, many things go wrong. We become hard to live with, we tend to be unkind, we find it easy to say cutting things and to hurt those around us. The same kind of thing is true if we fail to balance our diet or to supply our body with proper nutrition. If we do not daily exercise our bodies, they become soft and unable to keep up with the physical demands of life. The body will take advantage of an attitude of softness toward it.

It will also demand all of the pleasure it can get. Some bodies tend to demand excessive food, others various kinds of sexual pleasures that may be excessive or illegitimate. It is possible to have physical predispositions toward laziness, alcoholism, depression and many other undesirable things. But let me sound a warning. This is another point at which we are in danger of projecting blame. It is not ours to say, "Well, my body forces this upon me. I can't help myself." We cannot blame any sinful activity on "genes and chromosomes" or mom and dad.

A boy suffered brain damage in a wreck some years ago. His entire personality changed. He had been a bright, alert young man, easy to live with. But now he was the very opposite. His mother told me about something he had said, and then added, "I know that's not my boy talking. It's his messed-up system." Then she added something that showed she really understood: "But he's hidden behind the damage too long. Now he's got to accept help to get him back on the right road." That mother had found the true balance of the situation.

The psychological picture is closely related to the physiological one. This may be a third cause of weakness. Our minds in the present are influenced by the past. G. Campbell Morgan pointed out some sixty years ago, "a beginning is not a beginning."[1] When we try to make a new beginning in any area, we must acknowledge the past and deal with it. Even a beginning has a past.

Because of our past, we may be programmed favorably or unfavorably in regard to our spiritual needs and the requirements of God for our behavior. Francis Schaeffer has said, "Since the fall there is no truly healthy person in his body, and there is no completely balanced person psychologically."[2] Paul Tournier, Swiss physician and psychologist, concurs with Schaeffer when he says, "Psychological weakness is an obstacle to the spiritual life."[3] Tournier gives us a glimpse into his own personal struggles in a warm and human way:

> One of my closest friends is a Catholic colleague who leads a quite simple, straightforward and fruitful life. His childhood was happy, his development harmonious, his career brilliant. He never knew the feelings of inferiority and the tragic failures through which it was my lot painfully to forge my faith. In him obedience to God, victory over self, and benign authority over others seem to be easy and natural. He serves God and men with his strength as I try to serve them in spite of my weakness.[4]

Psychological imbalance affects our Christian lives in many ways: emotional extremes, false guilt, difficulty with grudges, pride, sexual problems, obsessions, fears and so on. We will never attain perfect balance in this life, but our progress can be substantial.

A fourth cause of weakness is simply our neglect of opportunities. We are like the father whose child receives an unassembled toy for Christmas. Sure that he understands its assembly at first sight, he flies into the task of putting it together. Finally, hopelessly stymied, he reads the instructions and undoes everything in order to do it as it should have been done the first time. This is such a common experience that a saying has crept into the language: When all else fails, read the instructions.

If we neglect attendance at the house of God, fellowship with his people, Bible study under sound leadership, and prayer, we can hope to be nothing but anemic at best. These are basic instructions, and we must be committed to doing these things and doing them well.

Numbness or insensitivity to the sinfulness of sin is a fifth cause of weakness. We all know that it is possible for a part of the body to lose feeling. A great cause of spiritual weakness in the twentieth century is a numbness to the seriousness of sin. I believe this condition has come about through a process of gradual conditioning that psychologists call "desensitization."

For example, some thirty years before this writing, a famous television talk-show host was reprimanded for using the term "water closet" on the air. Today one would notice the term only as being archaic. That is a harmless change, since only a false modesty made it offensive in the first place. But there are other topics and representations, the appearance of which in the public media should offend our sensibilities, and yet they no longer do. Imagine watching television in the 1950s, and then turning it off not to see it again until this evening. Can you conceive of the emotional shock to your moral values?

Why are we *not* shocked? Because we have been conditioned gradually to accept a slowly changing standard. We saw the first changes and learned to relax in their presence. This prepared us for the next change, and the next, until we are unshaken by things that would have shocked us beyond belief thirty years ago. Not only are we not shocked, we actually enjoy seeing them. We have become desensitized to the evil of what we are seeing.

E. M. Blaiklock of the University of Auckland in New Zealand wrote an article entitled, "The Breath of Hell." In it he describes this very process.

A young Englishman . . . was in Germany when the Nazis

degraded the Jews in the streets. At first he was sick at
the sight and rushed down a side street. The next time
he felt he could look, and stopped for a full minute. The
third time he watched. The fourth time, as he stood with
the jeering crowd, the sight seemed less revolting. He
was becoming, he told himself, "objective." And with this
came realization of his peril. This was not a part of life,
a social phenomenon for study. It was the breath of hell.[5]
In precisely this way we become numbed to the sinfulness
of sin. We usually become permissive along the lines of our
individual softness; some to greed, some to sexual affronts,
others to careless language, and so on. Alexander Pope
said it best of all when he wrote:

Vice is a monster of so frightful mien
    As to be hated needs but to be seen;
Yet seen too oft, familiar her face,
    We first endure, then pity, then embrace.

A sixth cause of weakness is *over*sensitivity—to self-interest.
Much of the weakness of modern Christians hinges on the
fact that we think of ourselves entirely too much. Our attention is forever being drawn to personal pain, inconven-
ience, violation of rights, acts directed against ourselves,
enjoyment of pleasure, and suffering from the unpleasant.
An epidemic of self-centered sensitivity seems to have
swept over the world. It is as though a protective covering
has been removed from nerves which were never intended
to be exposed. This heightened sensitivity to our own pleasures and pains has bred a vulnerability to many kinds of
temptation.

The removal of external restraint constitutes a seventh
cause of weakness. We cannot really know how strong we
are until the society around us says, "It's all right. Go ahead
and do what you want." With society saying that very thing,
we Christians are finding out just how strong we are . . . or
are not. We do not like to admit it, but social disapproval

has always been a strong deterrent to bad behavior. We would like to believe that we do right because of what we are, rather than because of what the folks around us expect us to be.

One sad example is the divorce rate. Christians have always believed that we must maintain united and stable homes because God willed it. But now that divorce is increasingly accepted, the rates among Christians are not far below those of the non-Christian population.

A tree that reaches maturity in the shelter of the forest has no trouble standing against the storm—as long as the forest remains. But if all the other trees are cut down and it is left alone, it is not as likely to survive a storm as the tree that grew up alone and developed certain internal strengths.

Like the tree with the forest cut down, Christians find themselves in a new position. In the face of weakened *ex*ternal restraint, the development of *in*ternal supports becomes even more important than it has been in the past. Our props have been snatched away from us and our true strength—or weakness—revealed.

D. Elton Trueblood has said of the present moral decay, "Conduct arises from lack of convictions." He continues, "The heart of the problem is what people believe or fail to believe. . . . If people do not believe that there are genuine values, they can have no answer to those who preach, 'All is permitted.' "[6] This, the eighth, is one of the chief causes of weakness before temptation. We are no longer sure what we believe. The kind of conviction that will restore our strength is the product of consistent Bible study and participation in a congregation that has conviction born of biblical understanding.

Our individual strengths may also be a cause of weakness. You may think that I have forgotten my subject. How can a strength be a weakness? When God gives special abilities to men and women, those abilities are always accompanied by special sensitivities. For example, we speak of the artist as a "sensitive" person. This sensitivity provides a special ability (a strength): to sculpt, paint, write or compose. But because the artist is especially sensitive, he or she may also be unusually sensitive to changes in mood and temperament. The very thing that gives ability may also lead to depression or pride. "The devil always attacks us on the points of our greatest strength."[7]

Look at an outstanding biblical example. David was a sensitive man. His accomplishments were great, and his sins were equally horrible. Alexander MacLaren observed of David, "His tremendously susceptible nature, especially assailable by the delights of sense, led him astray."[8] David was an artist who loved *beauty* of all kinds. Line, form and color affected him profoundly. Look at his poetry and you will see it. This was a gift of God—a true strength. But it was this very thing that made him so vulnerable to Bathsheba's great beauty (2 Sam 11:2).

He loved justice and generosity. David could not bear to see unfairness or stinginess. Obviously this gift enabled him to be a king who could rule with great justice and compassion: a true strength. But we tremble for him when we see how close to disaster this sensitivity brought him. In a rage, he rode out against the unfairness and miserly character of Nabal. Had it not been for the cool wisdom of Abigail, David would have committed murder.

David had a deep affection for his own family, certainly a proper thing that we all admire. But this affection, unbridled, led him into a foolish and weak mistake. Had it not been for the advice of his old friend, Joab, David would have lost his ability to govern through softness for his son (2 Sam 19).

Another application of this principle can be seen in the person with the sensitive conscience. We might think that a tender conscience would be the strongest defense against sin, but it is not. Thoroughly conscientious people can be induced to examine themselves in such minute and excessive detail that they come to utter despair. This is not at all uncommon. *Balance* is the watchword.

Finally, lack of motivation is a cause of weakness. A young woman who came to me for counsel was struggling with a deep guilt. She had been raised in a Christian home, but had become sexually promiscuous. She frankly admitted to me that she could not imagine life without the excitement of many lovers. She felt that there would be no sparkle or glow, and that all would become dull. She wanted to escape the guilt, and in some measure wanted to live as a Christian, but found it unthinkable to give up her sexual activity.

A friend said to me one day, "I don't want to be mature. It wouldn't be any fun."

Both of these people lack motivation. Each of us has times when we want to live right lives more than we do at other times. A graph of our motivation might look like a roller coaster. But the mature Christian is one who has moderated the highs and lows of motivation. Motivation has become an abiding act of the will rather than a fluctuating emotion.

Especially for the Weak

Some of you, like me, may seem to struggle more than others do with weakness in the face of temptation. In the previous paragraphs, *weakness* has been used to mean the absence of strength necessary to accomplish an assigned task. In the New Testament the Greek words translated *weakness* and *infirmity* literally mean "strengthless" and "not powerful."

New Christians especially may be disappointed to find that they do not have perfect control over their will. They may have heard others testify about their victories and have heard nothing about their failures. They may have experienced a "beginner's high" and gotten the impression that it's all going to "be a breeze." Suddenly, instead of a breeze, it's a gale that's blowing, and in their faces. As C. S. Lewis said, "We never find out the strength of the evil impulse inside us until we try to fight it."[9]

With the discovery of their limitations, new Christians need answers that will guide them through a period of disillusionment and start them up the ladder of growth in strength. One of the problems they may encounter is that of the inadequate answer. For example, somewhere I read this advice, "Make the decision to do right and the strength will be there to do it." That simply is not always true!

Here are some catch-phrases that characterize other poor answers: "You're trying too hard." "You're not trying hard enough." "You're depending too much on yourself." "You must let God live his life in you." "Let go and let God!" "Hang on!" "Believe!" "God has a miracle for you if only you will release your faith!"

The Strong Don't Understand

Some Christians are stronger than others. Those who are strong have found victory an easier matter, and these catch-phrases have worked for them. Almost any boost would have gotten them over the hump in the kind of battles they have fought. Christians with a reserve of balance and strength have never fought battles like those the weaker Christians fight. As a result, they really do not understand.

Of course, it is not their fault. They simply have never "been there." Dr. Samuel Johnson, the great lexicographer, said: "That fortitude which encountered no dangers, that prudence which has surmounted no difficulties, that integrity which has been attacked by no temptation, can at best be considered but as gold not yet brought to the test, of which, therefore, the true value cannot be assigned." I believe that many Christians who pass for being strong are simply untested. For example, the candy dish passes our friend and she politely refuses to take a piece. We say to her, "You've got real will power!" She answers, "No, I just can't stand the taste of toffee." She is not strong, only disinterested. Mark Twain put it in a more colorful way than Samuel Johnson when he said, "Anyone who has had a bull by the tail knows five or six things more than someone who hasn't."

We often have little empathy with those whose weaknesses, either in kind or degree, are unlike our own. We tend to believe that problems of the kind that we have never experienced are easy to solve, and the advice we give may be inadequate. Weaker brothers and sisters must have a complete answer, one that will help them build the defenses they need. In some cases this answer will include the help of a Christian professional who can assist with psychological problems that have muddied the spiritual waters.

Weakness Is No Excuse

God will make adjustments on the basis of innate weakness and strength when the rewards are handed out. But this does not mean that weaknesses are an excuse which gives us a sort of permission to go on sinning in the area of our problem. They are not excuses, because God has provided means whereby we can grow out of those weaknesses.

Perhaps you have been defeated in spiritual battle so often that you are ready to settle for defeat. Before you choose to do that, take these things into consideration: If you accept defeat, your spiritual usefulness will be hindered. A weak person is "like a city broken into and left without walls" (Prov 25:28). Not very flattering. Furthermore, yielding to temptation can bring about events that destroy business, family, personal respect and all hope for a stable future. Substantial strength will be gained only as you work to build walls against invasion, because it is God's plan that you become increasingly like him. Remember, we are "predestined to be conformed to the image of his Son" (Rom 8:29).

Causes of Strength

With such a phalanx of temptations about us, and so many causes of weakness, is there any hope of becoming strong? Yes, but only if we refuse to make excuses. John Milton said, "To excuse our faults on the ground of our weakness is to quiet our fears at the expense of our hopes."

We have good reasons to believe that in Christ we can become strong. For one thing, Jesus has true empathy for our weakness. He has always known each of your tendencies—all your weaknesses. Nothing you have ever done has surprised him. With full knowledge of your character, he has accepted you "in the Beloved" (Eph 1:6). He knows what it means to be dust (Ps 103:13-14), and has been tempted just as you are (Heb 2:17-18). This is the ladder's lowest rung; while others give instructions that you find impossible to follow, Jesus gives absolute understanding.

Jesus is so strong that he will accept no excuse for our remaining in a weakened state. He is strong enough to impart strength and direction to us. His understanding is a blade that cuts two ways: not only does he understand my infirmity, he also understands when I am only excusing myself. What *joy* to find a friend who understands me so well that I can never deceive him!

Another cause for hope is the promises of God. He has said that he would not leave us, and has promised help in temptation.

And we are not alone! Others have become strong after having been as weak or weaker than we are. Hebrews 11 tells us that through faith there were those who "won strength out of weakness" (v. 34). And they are cheering us on (Heb 12:1).

The order "gird up your loins!" is given in the Bible at least seven times. We know what it means to physically "gird up" our loins, but what does it mean in the spiritual sense? How do we do it? These seven references speak of at least three things: urgency (2 Kings 4:29; 9:1), courage (Job 38:3; 40:7; Jer 1:17) and preparation (1 Pet 1:13; Eph 6:14).

Girding up our loins means first of all to take courage. Second, it means to prepare. Third, the time is now. You cannot afford to wait until you feel like it. The writer of Hebrews flings down the gauntlet when he says, "Lift your drooping hands and strengthen your weak knees" (Heb 12:12). If the past has drained you of hope and courage, that hope and courage can come again. There is every reason to believe that it can!

Summary

While each of us has weakness, some have weaknesses so great that they despair of ever attaining spiritual victory. Partial answers lead only to further discouragement. The innately strong do not understand the problems of the weak and may be unable to give help. Adequate answers must be broadly based in the biblical strategy for over-coming.

Weakness may not be used as an excuse for sin. Answers do exist, and we are obliged to discover them through study, prayer and help from the body of Christ. On occasion the Christian brother or sister who can help us most is the one trained to deal with intricate psychological problems.

Weakness results from our fallen spiritual, physical and psychological natures, our neglected opportunities, our insensitivity to sin, our self-absorption, the weakening of external restraints, the loss of conviction, our special gifts being used against us, and our lack of motivation to do as we should.

Yet, for all this, there is hope in Christ because of his empathy, his refusal to accept our weaknesses as unchangeable, and his ability to lift us out of our plight. We also find hope in the examples of all those in the past who have become strong through God's grace.

Part Two
Solutions

4

Change Your Mind

"Truth professed has no transforming
power; truth received and fed upon
revolutionizes a man's whole character."
Alexander MacLaren

"Be transformed by the renewal of
your mind."
Paul (Rom 12:2)

GORDON TAYLOR, IN A FASCINATING book called *The Natural History of the Human Mind,* writes of a man suffering with cancer. The patient, whose case was reported in an English medical journal, told his doctor on a Tuesday that there would be no point in the doctor's returning on the Thursday following. He was going to die, he said, at 2:30 Wednesday afternoon. The day came and, with his family around him, "at 2:30 precisely he sighed, raised both hands above his head, smiled, and passed away."[1]

Lewis Thomas, M.D., is president of New York's Sloan-Kettering Cancer Center. Recently he wrote of a study of hypnosis used to remove warts.[2] Fourteen subjects with warts on both sides of their bodies were hypnotized and told that the warts on one side of their bodies would disappear. For nine of the fourteen, that is exactly what happened.

It is becoming obvious that the power of the brain to affect physical phenomena is stronger than we commonly imagine. In fact, the most dazzling frontier of science in the 1980s is not in outer space with its quasars and black holes. It is right here on earth, inside the cranial vault; it is the human brain. Composed of three brains, it contains perhaps as many as fourteen billion neurons in the cortex alone. It is a marvel of miniature circuitry, electrical activity, chemical compounds and mystifying reactions. And it consumes a third of the body's oxygen supply. We are indeed fearfully and wonderfully made.

Renew Your Mind

In part one we discussed the basic problem of temptation and its three sources: two outside ourselves and one within. Now we are ready to look at the solution, biblical principles for battle. The first of these is a change of mind.

We have already said that the solution is not in a technique, or a single, simple tactic to be applied in a crisis, though tactics sometimes have their place. Rather, the solution is the building of a strong Christian character that is ready for temptation before it comes.

But what is character? For the purpose of this book, we can say that it is the sum total of our personality; all that we think, believe, and feel; our reactions, mannerisms, habits, affections, values and tendencies which determine our external acts. All of this is centered in what the Bible calls the heart. Remember that in speaking of the heart, the Scripture says, "From it flow the springs of life" (Prov 4:23). In other passages it is called "mind," especially when emphasizing memory or purpose.

If our character is contained in the "heart" or "mind," then having strong spiritual character depends in some important way on what our minds are and what they contain. It is no wonder, then, that the Holy Spirit commanded through Paul, "Be transformed by the renewal of your mind" (Rom 12:2).

We might paraphrase Paul's words like this: "Change your behavior by changing your mind." A friend of mine who is well acquainted with computer programming told me that when a computer is reprogrammed, the programmer "dumps" the old program. This is something like what is to take place in the mind of the Christian: the old program "dumped" and a new one put in its place.

When we become Christians we become new creatures in terms of destination, purpose, devotion and allegiance. But that transformation is not total. Much yet remains to be changed; enough, in fact, to occupy us until death.

Deeper Than Thought

Deep in the subconscious mind, sin has its beginning. It is a thing of wonder that on an unconscious level, we actually devise plans and develop concepts that erupt into our awareness full grown. Some of us have worked on problems to which we could find no answer, only to have the solution come to us in a dream. This means that below the levels of awareness much is going on, and changing our minds in the sense that Paul spoke of it is something deeper than changing only our conscious thoughts.

But how can we change things about which we are not aware? Most folk who have tried to break a habit, no matter how small, have discovered that they are amazingly tenacious little vermin. Habits as insignificant as popping gum can hold tighter than barnacles to the hull of a ship; even more difficult are the habits of tobacco, alcoholism, sexual misbehavior, compulsive lying and others.

My mind is not always under my direct control. If I say, "Mind, change!" it does not always obey me. But I *can* do things that will in turn cause my mind to be acted upon by other forces. A crude illustration of this might be a piece of iron. Suppose I want a bar of iron to rust. I can't say, "Iron, rust," and expect it to happen. I can, however, rub a little salt on it, place it in a humid compartment of some kind and wait. Will it rust? Certainly it will.

I can deal with myself in the same way. The grace of God having been applied to my heart through salvation, I must now place my mind in a transforming atmosphere. By being in the right surroundings, exposing my mind to the right things, something happens: my mind changes! Slowly, perhaps, but it *does* change, somewhat like a sponge picking up liquid. This transforming atmosphere is not just a physical location such as a meeting place for Christians or a Bible college—though it could include both of these and certainly includes the first. Think rather in terms of an atmosphere that we create through our own actions. Beginning with this chapter we describe the actions that effect that change in the mind that is so necessary to transformed behavior.

Love the Lord
The first step following our salvation is to put God in the proper place in our lives. We must make Jesus Lord of all of life. We do not have one compartment that we call "religious" and another that we call "secular." "Whether you eat or drink, or whatever you do, do all to the glory of God" (1 Cor 10:31). He is Lord of your life as a working person, a parent, a sexual being, a friend, a watcher of television, a lover of life, as one who suffers, and as one who lives and dies.

This implies Christian love. In the 1800s, a Scottish preacher named Thomas Chalmers preached a sermon

that he called, "The Expulsive Power of a New Affection."
He said, "The best way of casting out an impure affection
is to admit a pure one; and by the love of what is good to
expel the love of what is evil. . . . We know of no other way
to keep the love of the world out of our heart than to keep in
our hearts the love of God."[3]

But as you think of Christian love, love for Christ, remember that the proper response to God's love for us is our
love for others (1 Jn 4:7-12). Remember too that this Christian love is different from what we normally think of as
love. As described in the New Testament, it is not primarily
an emotion, nor is it the same thing as affection. Rather,
it is a commitment to behave responsibly toward God and
others. The word *agape* and its derivatives refer to an intelligent act of the will, and its detailed description is found
in 1 Corinthians 13.

When Jesus said in Matthew 22 that we are to love God
with our whole being, he did not use the word for affection,
but the word for a decision to act responsibly. This means
that to love him in the way the Bible commands is exactly
the same thing as making him Lord.

How do I come to love God? Not by trying to work up
an emotion or by manipulating my affections, but simply
by making the decision that he will be Lord in my life, that
as he has become my Savior, he will also be my Lord. This
love is both a gift of God and a reasoned choice of the will.
It is implanted from above, accepted by choice and then
developed by repeated choices to love, sometimes in difficult situations.

We did not become what we are overnight. Our minds
are the products of our genetic inheritance, our environment, the examples after which we have shaped our lives,
the teachings we have been given, the chemistry of our
bodies, all our experiences and, most importantly, the specific choices that we have made as we faced each of these

things. We are in our minds what we have chosen and learned to be.

The implication, of course, is that we will not become what we ought to be in a few short days. Leighton Ford once said, "I used to think that God would deal with me like a grape, taking me all in one bite. But now I know that I am more like an onion, and that he is peeling me layer by layer." Ford is right. It took time for you and me to become what we are, a lot of time. It will take time for us to become all that God wants us to be and, most likely, it will take a lot of it. That is what our three score and ten is all about.

Summary
The mind is the key to all our behavior. Because it contains things contrary to God's plan, we are commanded to cause it to be renewed. If I am to act freely, if I am to resist temptation with joy and not grudgingly, I must change my mind, the very mainspring of my actions.

God's plan for the renewing of the mind is a reprogramming described in the Bible. If we expect to be overcomers, we must follow its instructions, beginning with making Jesus Lord of our lives. The mind's renewing is not an overnight phenomenon. The process will involve the rest of our lives. The chapters which follow are all about various aspects of the renewal of the mind.

5

Know What God Expects

"We never do evil so thoroughly
and heartily as when led to it by an
honest but . . . mistaken conscience."
Tryon Edwards

"What does the LORD require
of you . . . ?"
Micah (6:8)

IVAN PAVLOV WAS A NOBEL PRIZE winning scientist who once experimented with a dog and drove it crazy. Pavlov trained a dog to jump in one direction when shown a circle and to jump in another direction when shown an ellipse. If the dog responded correctly, it was given a reward of food.

When Pavlov had trained the dog thoroughly, he began to change the drawing of the ellipse, gradually making it less elliptical and more circular. In a short time the trained dog could no longer tell whether it was being shown a circle or an ellipse, and it was unable to respond appropriately. After so much of this kind of confusion, the dog simply lost its balance and reacted by biting its keeper, refusing food, becoming disobedient or lapsing into an unresponsive state of lethargy.

There is a human application of this experimental evidence: In order to live balanced, productive lives, we must know what is expected of us. This rule holds in the family setting, on the job, with our social contacts and in our relationship to God. Happily, God knows this need and has given us the basic code for human conduct. Summaries of this code include the Ten Commandments, the Sermon on the Mount and Jesus' command to love one another. Unhappily, as fallen creatures, we garble the messages badly, and even Christians often misunderstand what God really wants.

Nothing is more unsettling to us, nothing more discouraging, more demoralizing or more maddening than to be uncertain of how God's plan is to work out in our daily behavior. I should *never* become angry? Should there *never* be any conflict in my home? Am I never to *fight* for what I think is right? The questions are endless.

The Problem of Conscience

Some say that conscience answers these specific questions of conduct. But conscience can be wrong. It is as fallen as any other human faculty. It can make mistakes in spite of sincerity. It can be too lenient or too hard. It may make demands that are intolerable, require conduct that is too stringent, and be out of tune with God's expectations in a way that is a serious threat to a balanced life.

It is the person who suffers from a tyrannizing conscience that Paul discusses in Romans 14 and 1 Corinthians 8:7. He calls such a person a weak brother. While Paul does not say so, a tyrannizing conscience often produces pressures that make life an inner hell of unmet expectations.

Let's define *conscience* before we go further. It is that

human faculty which warns of anticipated violation or causes remorse when one has violated one's own system of right and wrong. The Holy Spirit makes use of it as a guide to conduct. But when the conscience is misinformed, the Holy Spirit is limited in his ability to direct the life.

It is true that there is probably no such thing as a perfectly trained conscience. But the problem can be remedied greatly when the believer studies the Scripture, worships in a balanced congregation and has teachers with good understanding of the Word. This is another step in renewing the mind.

Misconceptions

The rest of this chapter examines some common misunderstandings about God's requirements and then outlines what he *does* expect of us.

Some Christians have concluded that God requires absolute perfection. A casual reading of biblical references to perfection has led them to believe that at any given moment one can be totally free from sin. This is a misconception.

There are substantial reasons for believing that God does not expect perfection of us in this life. When the conscientious person realizes this, a heavy load is lifted and the conscience loses some of its power to tyrannize. Francis Schaeffer has said it most clearly: "We must not insist on 'perfection or nothing,' or we will end with the 'nothing.' "[1] Satan can destroy us with this twisted and unattainable ideal that we must be perfect in our fight against temptation.

To think that "if ten rules are good, a hundred are better" is another misconception. One group of Christians has made it a point to compile and frequently amend a list of prohibited things. Members of the group either abide by these rules or are excommunicated. Their goal is to have a perfect church "without spot or wrinkle." Here are some of the things forbidden: 1903, insurance; 1917, books and newspapers, courting; 1925, living in cities, nagging, laughing; 1930, musical instruments, novels; 1936, bobbed hair, fingernail polish, joking, talking about politics, giggling; 1939, automobiles, jazz, flesh-colored hose, joy rides to the beach or mountains, hanging out at filling stations on Sunday; 1945, wearing hats slanted, ghost or love stories; 1947, swimming pools; 1949, ruffled curtains, lace tablecloths; 1953, house plants, magazines such as *Country Gentleman, Life, Post* and *Boys' Life;* 1957, wedding cakes, four-part singing, television; 1961, curls, spike heels, using the term *kids;* 1965, basketball, tight dresses, bobby socks, root beer; 1968, cameras, flashy cars; 1969, miniskirts, shaving legs, long hair on men, loud colors.[2] And this is only a partial list.

I haven't included this in order to ridicule brothers in Christ. Instead I hope that readers will see the unreasonable lengths to which such things can go. Does Christ want us to live under this bondage? In the long run, does this help us resist temptation?

When Paul spoke of the weak brother who had too many scruples, he was talking about the person hedged about with these kinds of rules. Paul knew his subject well, for his old party, the Pharisees, were experts at making lists.

But isn't it helpful to have a rule for every situation that one might meet? No. Are these lists logical extensions of the commandments, or are they only extensions of our own fears and insecurities? I believe that they are created not out of a sense of security and faith in Christ, but out of our own terror of failure. According to Romans 14, large numbers of external rules do not indicate strength, but a lack of it. The solution to the problem is to develop strength of character, achieve spiritual and emotional balance, and stop appealing to rules that God did not ordain.

A third misconception is to think that deliverance from a besetting sin usually comes in an instant. Many Christians believe that they can have spiritual success, absolute peace,

great personal power and total victory over temptation—
instantly. It is only human to want the easy way, and it somehow seems more spiritual to find the sudden solution that
breaks through from the other world.

"But I have a friend who was instantly delivered from
drugs! What about him?" I did not say that there are
no special experiences, but that there is no standard experience available to everyone on request that will provide
instant and absolute deliverance. A friend of mine who had
come to Christ as a young man had grown cold and distant
and had finally begun to drink. One night he awoke in a
strange panic. He was beside himself and asked his wife,
"Joan, what can I do!" She said that they should pray.
So they got to their knees in the middle of the bed, and
he poured out his heart. Calm flooded his mind and he
slept.

From that time forward, alcohol was not the slightest
problem for him. The deliverance was real, sudden and
absolute. But God does not promise this kind of thing as a
standard experience to be expected by all his children.
Usually he works with us through a process.

Christians who pursue the "short cuts" may find spu-
rious solutions that work temporarily. Or they may find
"it" and then spend the rest of their lives making "it"
work. In the meantime they are totally diverted from
the real task of growing in grace, kept busy with mock
battles.

Working out our salvation is complex. We long for the
simple answer, the short cut, but there is no real progress
along that path. C. S. Lewis said: "If Christianity was something we were making up, of course we could make it easier.
But it is not. We cannot compete, in simplicity, with people
who are inventing religions. How could we? We are dealing
with Fact. Of course anyone can be simple if he has no facts
to bother about."[3]

What Does God Expect?

When God takes into account my fallen humanity and all that he knows about me, what does he really expect from me? What should my life be like on a day-to-day basis? The following overlapping principles are my answer to that question, based on biblical commandments.

God expects us to care how we behave. The Scripture says that we become new creatures in Christ Jesus (2 Cor 5:17). At the very least, this means that at conversion we begin to desire to do the right thing. And our motives begin to change. Robert Rudolph of Reformed Episcopal Seminary in Philadelphia said, "A Christian is one who has a long-term desire to please God." While our feelings may vary from time to time, and though we may sometimes be overwhelmed with contrary wishes, our long-term desire will be to live in a way that brings pleasure to God.

God also expects us to keep short accounts with him. When sin of any kind crops up, we are to admit that it has, and deal with it immediately (1 Jn 1:6-10). These short accounts are to extend not only to God, but to the people about us. I once heard Corrie ten Boom speak of walking in the light with others. She used the young woman who was her traveling companion as an example. Occasionally friction would arise between them. But as soon as it did, they dealt with it openly, honestly and with humility. Corrie called this "walking in the light with Connie."

God expects us to live in the present moment. Many evangelical Christians look back to an experience when Christ saved them. Others look to a moment subsequent to salvation when a deeper commitment was made. The event of the moment is an important thing, but "walking in the light" means ongoing, continuous improvement, not a single experience after which there is no change. Solomon said, "The path of the righteous is like the light of dawn, which shines brighter and brighter until full day" (Prov 4:18).

God expects our moral character to become increasingly like his. Paul tells us, "Be imitators of God, as beloved children. And walk in love, as Christ loved us and gave himself up for us" (Eph 5:1-2). We are to imitate God by imitating Jesus, who is God incarnate. "For those whom he foreknew he also predestined to be conformed to the image of his Son" (Rom 8:29). It is God's plan that we become more and more like him.

This implies a very important fifth principle: *God expects us to grow.* "Grow in the grace and knowledge of our Lord and Savior Jesus Christ" (2 Pet 3:18). As a boy in the fifth grade I was miserable. Most of the fellows my age weighed from 80 to 105 pounds, but I weighed 135. The problem of being overweight was compounded by the school itself. It was a country school—two rooms, forty-seven pupils, grades one through eight. It was in the heart of a blackjack oak woods in the Red River Valley of Texas. Most of the students' families eked out a living on tough, unproductive little farms. I was the city boy in the group, and this was my first year in the school. Tough country kids can make things pretty uncomfortable for overweight, backward city boys. That's exactly what some of them did for me.

The one that contributed most to my misery was an eighth grader named Jim Bob. He was taller, had been raised on a farm. It seemed to me that he was all muscle. A good share of his energy that year was dedicated to making my life a nightmare. I fought back as best I could, but sometimes that wasn't good enough.

The next two years brought a move to town and all the attendant changes of adolescence. The fat disappeared, exchanged for about six inches of new height and even some muscle. I welcomed those changes with more enthusiasm than anyone knew.

Then one night our family was out playing miniature golf, and whom should I meet but my old enemy, Jim Bob.

Jim hadn't changed at all. He was about the same height as when I had last seen him. But *I* was different! In fact, now I was taller than he was. There were no fights that night, and my old enemy acted like my old friend.

On the way home I felt good down inside. Someone for whom I had been no match, who had dealt me real misery, was no longer a threat of any kind. Why not? Nothing sudden and nothing dramatic, just growth. Normal growth reduced one of my most serious problems to nothing.

Normal *spiritual* growth will do the same kind of thing to our spiritual problems. If we realized this, rather than looking for the sudden and the spectacular, we would be more content with ordinary, unspectacular advances. A temporary defeat is not a long-term failure, but a stepping-stone to long-term growth.

God expects us to fight. "Let go and let God!" That has become popular advice. If one means by that advice, "Yield your will to God," I say Amen. On the other hand, if the meaning is, "Stop all effort to obey and let God do it all," I say, hold on just a minute!

The New Testament urges us to *strive* for self-control: "So run that you may obtain it [the prize]. Every athlete *exercises self-control* in all things. . . . I do not run aimlessly, I do not box as one beating the air; but *I pommel my body* and *subdue it,* lest after preaching to others I myself should be disqualified" (I Cor 9:24-27, italics added).

"I'm quitting! God must do it all!" is the wrong attitude. Renewing the mind is *divine* work, but it does not take place apart from *human* effort. We tend to confuse the gift of salvation, which is of grace and unearned by works, with sanctification. Sanctification is not substitutionary. It requires effort. Notice the beautiful balance of Scripture as it addresses this question: "Work out your own salvation . . . for God is at work in you" (Phil 2:12-13). *You* work because God is at work!

A number of years ago I bought a canoe and on vacation took it out onto a large lake. I had ignored the heavy clouds and distant thunder, and when I was far from shore the sky overhead darkened and rain began to fall. Lights on the warning buoys began to flash, and the wind blew with tremendous force. At this crucial moment I could have prayed for deliverance, or I could have begun to paddle for shore. I chose to combine my options by praying hard and paddling like crazy. Passivity was inappropriate to the circumstances. It is also inappropriate in spiritual warfare. Yes, there will be moments when our only option is to pray. But as we meet temptation, generally, we must pray and work.

Finally, *God expects our conduct to be an example to the world.* Paul told the church at Philippi, "Do all things without grumbling or questioning, that you may be blameless and innocent, children of God without blemish in the midst of a crooked and perverse generation, among whom you shine as lights in the world" (Phil 2:14-15). And we may be encouraged just as the Philippian Christians must have been, when Paul said to them, "I am sure that he who began a good work in you will bring it to completion at the day of Jesus Christ" (Phil 1:6). For Jesus gave himself for us in order "to redeem us from all iniquity and to purify for himself a people of his own who are zealous for good deeds" (Tit 2:14).

Summary

Being uncertain of what God wants of us breeds emotional and spiritual imbalance. But our consciences are easily misled and must be trained (or retrained) by careful study of Scripture.

We must beware of several misconceptions: that God requires absolute perfection, that we must hedge ourselves in with many rules, and that spiritual deliverance usually comes in an instant.

God expects at least the following things from us: that we care how we behave, that we keep short debit accounts with him, that we live in the present, that our moral character become increasingly like God's, that we grow, that we fight, and that our conduct be an example to the world.

6

Know Your Enemy

"Fore-warned, fore-armed."
Cervantes

"For we are not ignorant of his devices."
Paul (2 Cor 2:11 KJV)

THE HUMAN RACE SADLY HAS demonstrated real genius for discovering new methods for fighting and killing. The long list began millennia ago with the club. As time has passed, weapons have increased in sophistication: the bow and arrow, armor and chariots, catapults, men-of-war, cannon and tanks, poison gas and bombs, chemical and germ devices, now the dreaded atomic weapons, and tomorrow perhaps death- and disorientation-rays.

Strange as it may seem, some very efficient war machines have been banned from use. The Hague Conference of 1907, the Geneva Protocol of 1925 and the Geneva Conventions of 1929 have all produced agreements by which the nations fight wars in a somewhat more humane way. Nerve gas, biological germ contrivances and bullets that expand upon impact are all prohibited, since they produce more suffering and death than the conferees believed necessary.

In spiritual war, however, there are no rules. God sometimes restrains Satan (Job 1—2), but there seem to be no weapons which he cannot use at one time or another. Nothing is too cruel, and nothing is sacred to him.

Satan's Devices

Paul wrote to the Corinthian church about a congregational member who was practicing incest. He told the church that it should take disciplinary action (1 Cor 5). In his second letter to Corinth, Paul refers to the church's discipline (which seems to have produced repentance) and tells the members that they should not press the matter further. For if they do, the penitent member will likely be crushed with excessive sorrow (2 Cor 2). He tells them to forgive him, for if they do not, Satan will gain an advantage over them, "for we are not ignorant of his devices" (2 Cor 2:11 KJV).

Put another way, Paul is saying that we know how Satan operates, and thus informed, we are better able to stay out of his traps. "Fore-warned, fore-armed." But could Paul say of *us* that we are not ignorant of Satan's devices? What are they?

Jesus' wilderness temptation illustrates one of Satan's devices: he chooses special times to attack. In the wilderness temptation the devil confronted Jesus in order to lead him into sin. When he failed, he gave up and left. The Scripture says an interesting thing: "And when the devil had ended every temptation, he departed from him *until an opportune time*" (Lk 4:13).

Satan and his devils are not always present with us. But when we are vulnerable for some reason, he will be there. His attack will be at an opportune time.

Think of Jesus' most difficult moments. The wilderness temptation was a special opportunity for the devil for several reasons. First of all, Jesus had just heard the voice of God say, "This is my beloved Son, with whom I am well pleased" (Mt 3:17). This must have been an emotionally high time for him, and emotional highs are times when we are more easily misled.

Besides that, he was alone. Without the restraining influence of friends we may act in ways that we would be ashamed of if they were around. In loneliness we may become depressed and look for solutions to our loneliness that are unacceptable. Standing alone against social pressure, we may yield.

And Jesus was hungry. "Deprivation increases drive" is a rule that applies to all of our physical appetites. When our needs are unmet for an extended period, the internal drive to fulfill the need mounts up and we feel increasing pressure. This applies to hunger, sleep, thirst and other needs and desires. As the pressure builds, we become less and less concerned about whether the need is met in a legitimate way.

This was a crucial time in Jesus' ministry. The entire plan demanded absolute success over all temptation. Knowing that must have made this a time of great emotional stress. We also have times of emotional stress. Our balance may be challenged by as simple a thing as too little sleep or as profound a thing as a death in the family, an injury or illness, financial loss or a change in occupation.

Obviously, we cannot avoid all stress. That would not even be desirable. But we can begin by recognizing that some periods of time are more dangerous than others. We can also take better control of our own lives—the amount of sleep we get, the food we eat, the worrying we do.

That we can do all things through Christ does *not* mean that we are to invite trouble by mismanaging our lives. This is important: we are not to create the devil's opportunities for him. Neither should we create the devil's opportunities in the lives of others. The apostle Paul tells married couples, for example, that they are to be good sexual partners. He says that depriving husband or wife of regular sexual intercourse creates a special opportunity for Satan to lead the partner into infidelity (1 Cor 7:3-5).

Paul warns parents also about leading their children into temptation (Eph 6:4). He says that fathers are not to be unreasonable in their discipline, thus provoking anger in their children. Many other possibilities in family and social life will come to mind as you think about this.

Implying that God is a liar is another of Satan's devices. At Jesus' baptism, God's voice was heard saying, "This is my beloved Son" (Mt 3:17). In the wilderness, the devil turned this into "*If* you are the Son of God..." (Mt 4:6), implying that God had lied. This is exactly what Satan did to Eve when he said to her, "Did God say...?" (Gen 3:1). He went ahead to cast other shadows on God's character by telling Eve that God had ulterior motives in requiring her obedience (Gen 3:5).

He's still doing the same thing: "Is God really there?" or "Can the Bible be trusted?" Most of us have been tempted along such lines. It is an encouragement to know that stable Christians are tested with doubts occasionally. C. S. Lewis said in a letter,

> Now that I am a Christian I do have doubts in which the whole thing looks very improbable: but when I was an atheist I had moods in which Christianity looked terribly probable. This rebellion of your moods against your real self is going to come anyway. That is why Faith is such a necessary virtue: unless you teach your moods

"where they get off," you can never be either a sound Christian or even a sound atheist, but just a creature dithering to and fro, with its beliefs really dependent on the weather and the state of its digestion. Consequently one must train the habit of Faith.[1]

Another of Satan's tactics is accusation. In Revelation 12: 10, Satan is called "the accuser of the brethren." The prophet Zechariah had a dramatic vision in which he saw Joshua the high priest dressed in filthy clothing, standing before the angel of the Lord. The devil stood at Joshua's right hand making accusations to God against him (Zech 3:1-3).

There are at least two ways in which Satan accuses Christians: first, for real sins we have committed, but which are under the blood of Christ, and second, by making some act or motive of ours appear to be sin when it is not. We all know what it is to feel guilt for real sin—an altogether proper thing. But when that sin has been confessed to God we must refuse to carry the load of guilt any longer, refuse to listen to Satan's accusations. We may still be ashamed, but not guilty. A psychologist friend of mine asks his clients, "Who do you think you are, refusing to forgive yourself when God has forgiven you?" Because of Christ's death and resurrection, Satan is unable to successfully lodge a complaint against a penitent believer at the throne of God. But if we do not remember this, Satan can make life very miserable for us.

The second possibility is also a very serious one. He will accuse us by leading us to believe that some things are sin which are not. For example, think of the young man who has read Matthew 5:27 and 28: "You have heard that it was said, 'You shall not commit adultery.' But I say to you that every one who looks at a woman lustfully has already committed adultery with her in his heart." Remember that Satan can quote Scripture too. Many an earnest young

Christian has read this passage and made a crucial mistake. He has taken *lust* to mean "admire" or "enjoy the beauty of" or "be stirred by." Of course *lust* doesn't mean any of those things. *Lust* means to want for oneself, in this case for sexual purposes. A normal Christian male will enjoy the beauty of a woman, even be stirred by it, but because of proper self-discipline will not imagine himself in bed with her. He will not want her for himself.

Amazingly, Satan can prevent the difference between these two things—lust and admiration—from ever entering the young man's head. This means that if he is sexually normal and is also a conscientious Christian, he is likely to spend the rest of his life with a sense of guilt about what he feels when a beautiful woman walks by. If he concentrates on avoiding such sights—sights which cannot be avoided in our society—and if he refuses to acknowledge these normal feelings, he is likely to develop a psychological compulsion toward voyeurism. In other words, this is a tactic by which Satan uses the strong desire of the Christian to be faithful, combined with a misunderstanding of Scripture, to lead him into discouragement that can destroy him. I am convinced that much sexual sin in adult life is the bursting forth of the great pressures caused by such false guilt.

Another of Satan's tactics is to lie—telling *just enough of the truth to make the fatal lie believable.* He even quotes Scripture. One example of this is the current interest in life after death. Satan seems to be saying to people, "All right, I'll give you that point. There *is* life after death. Now, let's look into it a bit further." And with that, many people have sought to contact departed loved ones and have pursued similar investigations.

A small satanic lie can do massive damage. Botulism is an acute food poisoning. The toxin involved is the most powerful biological poison known. Its minimum lethal dose is 0.00003 micrograms per kilogram of body weight of the

30 picograms   3×10⁻¹¹ grams

victim. One authority said, "That is almost equivalent to having a flea on a freight train which is 100 miles long, and when the flea gets on, it derails the entire train."[3] Satan's lies are like that.

Promoting imbalance is another device of Satan. In some of the preceding points we have touched on this. An acquaintance of mine told me this story: Late one night, he and his twin brother were making a long trip by car, his brother driving as my friend slept. Suddenly he woke to the sound of "tic . . . tic . . . tic." His brother had gone to sleep at the wheel, and the car, moving at a high rate of speed had drifted to the right until the heads of the rivets holding the highway guard rail to the posts were "ticking" the fender of the car as it flew past.

My friend had the presence of mind to know that even in this desperate situation he could not afford to startle his sleeping brother, for, wakened suddenly, he would be likely to jerk the wheel sharply to the left and roll the car. So he reached out gently and eased the wheel to the left, away from the guard rail, took firm hold on the wheel and quietly spoke his brother's name. All was well, but those were breathless moments.

When we stray from the path, Satan will try to make the situation fatal by prompting us to "jerk the wheel to the left." If Satan cannot draw us subtly off balance in one direction, he will push us suddenly to the other. In many cases, people do not thoughtfully *choose* to sin. The sin comes as a reflex response. The tempting thing is there so suddenly, so unexpectedly, that it takes them by total surprise and stands before them as a seemingly irresistible force. The young couple in love may not set out to have sexual intercourse, but one small thing leads to another until passions are so high that there is no turning back. Perhaps you did not set out to argue with your dad; but he took what you said in the wrong way, and before you knew it, you were both angry.

Paul admonished, "Keep alert with all perseverance" (Eph 6:18). To be alert is to be awake, thinking, praying, studying, evaluating life and our surroundings honestly. So "keep alert."

Of course Satan has other methods, many of which are implied in other chapters of this book. He brings pain; he appeals to our capacity for enjoyment; he divides Christians one from the other, and he even divides them internally against themselves. This side of heaven there are no final guarantees that we will not be tripped by one of his tricks. It is not that the defenses provided to us are inadequate, but that we are merely human and fail to use them properly. Thankfully, the blood of Christ cleanses us from all sin; and thankfully, we can become better and better prepared for what we face. Besides that, we are grateful to remember that in the end Satan will have no access to us in any manner. He will be unable to accuse us either before God or ourselves. He will be unable to trick us, throw us off balance or otherwise assault us.

Summary

Satan will stop at nothing. Among other things, he uses the following tactics: 1. He chooses his own time of attack, our weak moments. 2. He casts aspersions on the character of God. 3. He accuses us. 4. He lies. 5. He promotes imbalance.

These attacks must be met with humility and dependence on Christ for strength. It is our job to be sure that we do not provide Satan more opportunities than necessary.

7

Walk by
the Spirit

"The continuing fullness of the Spirit
manifests itself in moral qualities."
John R. W. Stott

"Walk by the Spirit, and do not
gratify the desires of the flesh."
Paul (Gal 5:16)

ON THE MORNING OF September 4, 1665, the streets of
London were empty. The stillness stretched from the poor-
est backstreet to the avenue on which the palace sat. One
could walk Lumber Street and meet not more than twenty
persons from one end to the other. The noise of business
was gone; the only sound was the constant tolling of church
bells. Shops were closed. Grass grew in the streets. The
door of an occasional house was marked with a red cross
and the plea, "Lord, have mercy upon us." Open spaces
often contained great mounds of earth many yards long
and underneath the mounds were the bodies of London's

dead. Among those not dead and dying, as many as could moved away from the festering city.

Beginning with the warmth of the previous spring, the Londoners had seen dead rats lying about in houses, streets, public buildings and along the wharfs. Shortly after, one and then another of the people came down with high fever. They grew pitifully weak, felt a chill, and before long their heads seemed nearly to burst with pain. Some went insane as the bacteria attacked the brain. Screams and weeping filtered from the houses of the wealthy and poor alike. Between the third and sixth day of the illness, the victim would die.

As the weather grew warmer and the filth of the street's open sewers renewed its putrid bacterial life, the death toll climbed higher. In one late summer week alone, seventy-four hundred died. Ox carts were driven through the streets at night, their drivers calling, "Bring out your dead!" The numbers of dead was so great that they were buried in common graves.

As autumn came on, the death toll mercifully dropped, and many of those who had fled the city came home. But when spring came again, the plague returned. June, July and August brought a repeat performance of the summer before. But on September 2, 1666, everything changed.

On Pudding Lane, a maid who worked for a baker brought in the night's kindling and, before going to bed, piled it near the fireplace—too near. In the early morning hours the baker awoke to the smell of smoke and found the shop ablaze.

The wind was high and from the northeast that night, and the flames leapt from house to house, eating up block after block. The fire swept through the town, taking the greatest buildings of the city, including St. Paul's Cathedral. The huge building's stones exploded with the heat, and the lead roof ran like water from the gargoyies' mouths and molded itself between the steaming cobblestones of the streets.

The fire raged until September 6, when it finally burned itself out. In those five days it consumed thirteen thousand houses, eighty-nine churches, the Royal Exchange and most of the company halls. Across the Thames, the people of London were sprinkled with ash and cinder as they watched all they owned go up in the "horrid, malicious, bloody flame."

Their homes and shops were gone; that was true. But the "horrid, malicious, bloody flame" had done them a service. Also gone was the plague. The flames had licked the putrefaction from the sewers, ferreted the bacteria from its deepest place of hiding and destroyed the houses that had been built so close together that no sunlight could reach the streets. All with a loss of only six lives. London was rebuilt, and its people regained their health. The only voice capable of answering the bubonic plague had spoken.

Another Fire
During the Jewish Feast of Weeks, shortly after Jesus' death and resurrection, the Christian church was born. On that day the Holy Spirit came upon one hundred twenty disciples of Jesus of Nazareth who were waiting in an upper chamber in a Jerusalem house. From that moment on, all true believers have been indwelled by the Holy Spirit of God.

The one visible symbol of his coming that day was fire. And this is the only fire capable of answering the plague of sin, of "binding the strong man" (Mt 12:29) who is our Adversary. John Peter Lange says of this event: "The Holy Ghost is a divine fire, purifying the heart, consuming all that is sinful in it, elevating it to God, and sanctifying it."[1]

Without the Holy Spirit, the Christian could not receive God's cleansing work. Humanly, we can do no more than reform ourselves. And more often than not, we are unable to do even that. But the fire of the Spirit pulls down old buildings, boils out putrefaction and lets the sunlight into the narrow streets of our once shadowed and plague-ridden hearts.

What does the Spirit do to help us with temptation? First, he actually takes up residence within. This is a mystery, but totally real. He places his validating seal on our relationship to God (Eph 4:30), gives assurance of salvation(Rom 8:16), opens our understanding to the Scriptures (1 Cor 2:10-13), guides us in questions and choices (Rom 8:14), prays on our behalf (Rom 8:26), and lastly, "wars" against the flesh (Gal 5:17).

What Do I Do?
As the Spirit has obligated himself to us, we have a recip-rocal obligation to him. Once the fire of the Spirit has been kindled by saving grace, we are to tend that fire just as we would tend a campfire. We feed, stoke and stir it. The Scripture calls this tending of the fire "walking by the Spir-it" (Gal 5:16). Several things are involved.

First, the mind must be set on the things of the Spirit. That is, we must be concerned with his will, his Word and the way in which his Word is to be worked out in our be-havior. Second, the body must be dedicated to him (Rom 12:1). It is his temple. But this does not mean that we no longer have a private, personal life with options, choices and joys. God is no tyrant. Third, we must trust all of life to him. Romans 1:17 tells us that the just *live* by faith. And fourth, we must obey him. These four things are far from exhaustive, but they are basic to walking in the Spirit.

Another important element in walking in the Spirit is the command to be "filled with the Spirit." There is much con-fusion among Christians about what this means. But make no mistake about it, it is a command! What does it mean?

First of all, the tense of the verb indicates a continuing action. *The Amplified Bible* renders the passage, "but ever be filled.... " (Eph 5:18). It is not a matter of having been filled once and never needing further filling. Rather, it is a matter of remaining at the fountain constantly.

Fullness and obedience are of one cloth. At any given moment the believer is filled with the Spirit to the exact degree that he or she is obedient and trusting. To the degree that a person is *dis*obedient, harboring unforgiveness, lack of love, resentment and contentiousness; to the degree that this person loves some thing, person or wish above God; to the degree that illegitimate activity allows space within the heart and life to be taken by that which is not of God—to that degree, she or he is not filled with the Spirit.

Our Continual Need

I once heard of a preacher who was so carried away that he mixed his metaphors like this: "O Lord, you have begun your work in us. The spark of the Spirit is glowing in our hearts. Now, Lord, water that spark!" That mistake is easy to make because of the biblical metaphors of fire and filling. I began speaking of the Spirit as fire; I now want to emphasize the need to be constantly filled as with water.

In the Great Plains states where I live, the prairies seem endless. Bordered on the east by America's woodlands and on the west by the Rocky Mountains, the plains stretch south into Mexico and north into Canada. This is the great cattle country of the North American continent.

Across these high plains there are large expanses where there is no sign of water. But here and there, wells have been drilled and old-fashioned windmills stand above them, bringing the underground springs to the surface. Beside the windmill usually stands a tank of galvanized steel, about three feet deep and from six to fourteen feet across. A pipe runs from the pump over the edge of the tank, and a small stream of clear, cold water, pulsing with the rise and fall of the pumping rod, flows in. The mills are generally unattended, pumping whenever there is wind, which is most of the time.

Fly over these grazing grounds and you will see cattle paths leading from nowhere to the tanks, like spokes radiating from the hub of a wheel. The cattle have learned where to find the life-giving water. They come and drink as they wish, for the tank is always full and usually overflowing just a little.

There is often life in the tank—algae, frogs—and, in the mud around it, water puppies. Often, in the drier seasons, the windmill tower marks a spot of green on the rolling prairies of dry, beige grass. All of that life depends on the constancy of the breezes, the working order of the mill, the openness of the pipe, the presence of underground water and the tank's availability to receive the continuous flow. If the pump rod breaks or the large fan is destroyed by too much wind, if the pipe becomes clogged or the leathers on the rod wear out, the flow stops. The water stagnates, the tank becomes empty, the algae, frogs and water puppies die, and the cattle have nothing to drink.

This is very much like the working of the Holy Spirit. The "water" is always there, his "breezes" always blowing. It is the keeping of our mill, pump, pipe and tank in good order, free to pump and to receive the flow, that is our responsibility.

If the flow stops, life quickly stagnates, our tank empties and the life around us, so dependent on our spiritual vitality, begins to wither. When this happens, we are in no condition to fight battles in the heavenly realms.

Summary

The Holy Spirit, symbolized by fire, makes our cleansing possible. Christians are inhabited by the Spirit, but must appropriate his work of cleansing and warring against temptation.

We have an obligation to tend the fire and walk by the Spirit. This includes setting our minds on the things of the Spirit, allowing him to work at our mind's renewing, dedicating our bodies to him, trusting him, and obeying him.

The Spirit has commanded us to be filled with himself. So the question becomes not "How much of the Holy Spirit do I have?" but "How much of *me* does he have?"[2]

8

Build Your Walls

"No man is free who cannot
command himself."
Pythagoras

"The fruit of the Spirit is
... self-control."
Paul (Gal 5:22-23)

"MARRIAGE SHOULD NOT HAVE to be work. You fall in love,
get married, and that's it."[1] Because he thought so, the
divorce was almost inevitable.

In the same way, that person can never be spiritual who
believes "following Jesus should not have to be work," for
this idea is a romantic misconception. Following Jesus is
work, and that work is called "self-discipline."

Self-discipline requires will power. A peanut-butter
cookie with a big chocolate candy kiss sitting in the center
melts my will power as though it were butter in a hot skillet.
So do a few other things. Will power is the ability to refuse

to do a wrong thing, or to choose to do a right thing.

Psychologists tell us an interesting thing about will power. They say that our "midbrain" is the seat of all our drives and emotions: hunger, thirst, sex, joy, anger and others. These are pure drives without any kind of restraint. The "roof brain" or cerebral cortex, which does our reasoning and thinking, is responsible for keeping the midbrain in line. Without the cortex's restraint, it would literally run away with itself.[2]

We say, "She was carried away with rage," or "He lost his head over that girl," or "She wanted to do it so badly that she just was not thinking clearly." It's true. We really can "lose our heads." The midbrain becomes the temporary master as the storm of raw drive blots out reasonable restraint. This sounds very much like Robert Lewis Stevenson's "Dr. Jekyll and Mr. Hyde," doesn't it? The idea is the same, and the outcome is the same. Mr. Hyde was not fit to live in society because of his unrestrained life. Self-restraint is necessary to live in society and to live as a Christian.

Walls Torn Down
In A.D. 70 the Roman armies were camped around Jerusalem. Their siege was part of the most dramatic battle of world history. Even with eighty thousand soldiers, Titus was unable to take the city because of its strong walls and determined defenders. A thousand years before the siege of Jerusalem, Solomon understood perfectly the value of walls, and he understood the fate of cities whose walls were broken down. He also knew that a person "without self-control is like a city broken into and left without walls" (Prov 25:28). Any sin can get into an undisciplined life. There is no resistence. We would say that such a person has no will power. The walls which defeated the Roman siege were there long before the Romans attacked. Similarly, the spiritual battle has been won or lost before tempta-

tion ever comes knocking, depending on whether we have built protective walls against it.

Would your life be different right now if you had exercised more self-control in the past? Was there a time when your anger destroyed the closeness you had with your wife, your husband, parents or friend? Has some outburst thrown your Christian testimony in doubt? Or is there a threat of some such thing if you do not change? How could self-discipline make your future more secure?

Think of the freedom of being without your besetting sin: alcohol, excessive food, too much sleep, whining, complaint, worry or temper. Imagine how life would be without the guilt, the damaged relationships or the expense of your sin. When the walls are broken down we are neither what we want for ourselves, nor what God wants for us.

How Do We Become Disciplined?

A woman wrote to a popular answer column and asked, "What can a mother say to a 14 year old girl who is spoiled, disobedient, disrespectful and who screams, 'I know I'm a rotten kid but it's your fault. You raised me'?"

The answer was, "Dear Mother: Untie your tongue and tell your daughter, 'Yes, I raised you and I'm sorry I didn't do a better job. If you don't like the way you are, then make something better of yourself. People can change if they are willing to work at it. Be my guest.' "[3]

She was right. Most people can make basic changes in themselves that will improve their lives. How much greater opportunity the Christian has, working hand in hand with God! We even have the specific promise, "The fruit of the Spirit is . . . self-control" (Gal 5:22-23).

Once, while musing over Proverbs 25:28, I asked, "Lord, what can a person in such a condition do?" The thought came instantly, "Why, rebuild the walls." Of course! That is exactly what one must do. But then I asked, "How are they rebuilt?" The simple answer is: "Stone by stone." Walls don't just happen. They are built one stone at a time.

What are these walls? You may expect that I will answer prayer, Bible study, faith and other pious disciplines. Those are vital, but I leave them to another chapter. The walls that I am now talking about are less obvious, *seem* less spiritual, but are just as important. In fact, though you may read your Bible and pray constantly, without these walls you will fail.

Understanding

The first wall is understanding. Scripture constantly presses us toward clearer understanding of God and his expectations, Satan and his methods, of the people around us, our mates, our children and of all of life. The greater our understanding, the better our chances of knowing how to respond when the chips are down.

We acquire understanding by being students, through prayerful study of the Bible and of life, through asking many questions, knowing whom to ask and to whom to listen, and being attentive in the hard school of experience. We must work at it, develop a taste for understanding, hunting for it as for hidden treasures (Prov 2:4). John Locke displayed the kind of attitude which we ought to have when he said, "I attribute the little I know to my not having been ashamed to ask."

Balanced Emotions

The second wall is balanced emotions. Emotions are not easy to analyze. They are a part of us, but they are our least consistent part. They influence our judgment enormously, but they are the least trustworthy of all influences. Without them we would be flat, uninteresting and uninterested, featureless in personality. Without them we would have little drive, and we would not know the pleasure of excitement. Emotions are a blessing and a curse, useful tools and hindering roadblocks, helpful and detrimental, icing on the cake and gall in the meat.

Each of us knows someone whose emotions are strong and close to the surface like a floating mine with detonators protruding in all directions. Family and close friends must navigate cautiously, walk on tiptoe or as if on eggs, always guarding what they say or one of the detonators will be touched and an enormous explosion will rend the home, church or social group.

On the other hand, there are people who have strong emotions, but have made them their slave rather than their master. These people consciously put emotions to work. They control their speech and actions, burn off frustration with vigorous physical activity, talk about valuable ideas rather than about other people, channel excitement into projects, and use reason and love to kill out resentment and bitterness. They have attained a state of evenness—always *This is a fantasy* ready with a smile, rarely depressed, usually approachable, kind, happy—yet also able to shed tears of compassion without being eaten up by sorrow. Interested in the universe and what it contains, they know little about boredom. Life for them has a deep undercurrent of joy based on a secure relationship with Jesus Christ. Such people have consciously and wisely built a wall against temptation.

Here are some axioms about emotion that are good to remember. <u>Emotions should serve the intellect and the soul, never rule them.</u> Emotion opens up a path by which truth may reach the mind. But emotion is a deceiver and will sometimes try to masquerade as truth itself. Emotion may assist the intellect in making its decisions, but ought never to be allowed to make decisions on its own. A state of high emotion is no more spiritual than a clear-headed state; the Spirit of God uses them both, but he uses intellect far more than emotion. Decisions should be made when the fires of passion are banked; a good decision made in the heat of emotion is either a stroke of luck or God's special care for the fool. Emotions have a purpose and are to be enjoyed and used wisely.

But what if your emotions are in charge? You have little self-control, and your basic drives tend to take over. Psychologists sometimes measure a person's maturity by the ability to postpone pleasure. For example, the child may say, "I want a candy bar." Mother answers, "It's too close to dinner time. We will eat dinner and afterward you may have something much better than the candy—a bowl of ice cream with strawberries." But the little one cries and insists on the inferior pleasure now, rather than being glad to wait.

There are many adult Christians who are just like that. God offers us a much greater pleasure in the future if we will resist the inferior pleasure now. But in our foolish immaturity, we demand instant gratification. This pattern has as many applications as there are human drives. One of the best biblical examples is Esau, who sold his birthright for a mess of pottage.

If your emotions are in control and the desire for immediate gratification overwhelms you, if you are unable to make headway against this pattern, you may need help from an outside source. Your life probably will not stabilize until you receive it, or until you reach declining years and the normal passions of life begin to lose their appeal to you.

Remember: If a commitment to Jesus Christ is based on our feelings alone, it *cannot* be consistent. There will be some days when our emotions dictate devotion to Christ and other days when they dictate devotion to something else. We must become their masters or all hope for a steady life is lost.

Positive Joy
The third wall is positive joy. We have already said that

emotions can be our ally. The emotion of joy can be a wall to keep sin out. Nehemiah said, "The joy of the LORD is your strength" (Neh 8:10). What is the joy of the Lord? It is an altogether wholesome emotion that springs from dwelling on the fact that all is well between you and God.

Philippians 4:8 is the key to the Christian's development of personal joy: "Finally, brethren, whatever is true, whatever is honorable, whatever is just, whatever is pure, whatever is lovely, whatever is gracious, if there is any excellence, if there is anything worthy of praise, think about these things."

I like that word *dwell*. It carries a certain calmness with it that appeals to me very much. In this case, *dwell* means more than to think about these things. It means to think about them and to *keep on* thinking about them.

Here is an illustration of the effect of Paul's advice. All my life I have been afraid of heights. If I climb a windmill or other tower, I can only hang on for dear life. But several years ago I went mountain climbing. The first day out, the man who led the climb insisted that we practice rappelling, going from the top of a cliff to the bottom by lowering ourselves down its face on a rope. We were going to rappel on a one-hundred-ten-foot cliff. How could I ever manage to do it with my fear of heights?

It would have been possible to think of the one hundred ten feet to the bottom of the cliff or of the fact that ropes sometimes break or knots come untied. Of course I knew all of those things, and if I had chosen to *dwell* on them, it's doubtful that I could ever have backed over the edge. But there was another possibility: to think of the strength of the rope, the skill with which it was made, the strength of the tree trunk, the long experience of the man who was directing every move.

What actually happened was that I was so impressed by the positive elements of the situation that I had no problem at all and was able to back over the cliff's edge and make a successful rappel. In fact I enjoyed it and did it many times after that! Dwelling on the security of the rappel device gave me real peace of mind, a feeling of safety and calm.

The Christian life is like that. We don't ignore the difficulties, we take them into account and deal with them carefully and courageously. But we do not *dwell* on them. Instead, we dwell on the sufficiency of God. We look at what he has done for others and for us in the past. When we do this, we find the joy of security, and we build a wall, establish a positive emotion and find a new defense against temptation. Remember what Nehemiah said, "The joy of the LORD is your strength."

Experience

The fourth wall is experience. Books are written so that we might learn from another's experience. We are taught by our parents for the same reason. Yet, often we hear the advice, think we understand and then discover in the clutch that we did not understand at all.

Samuel Taylor Coleridge said, "Experience is not transmissible." I think he may have been right. We do not know precisely what a hot horseshoe is until we pick one up with our bare hands; but when we do, the information becomes ours quickly and at the deepest level. There is no substitute for learning by doing, for trying and failing, for testing and finding what works and what doesn't. I do *not* mean that a commandment should be broken in order to see what will happen. The point is that good advice becomes better when we practice it. And when we do some foolish thing, the consequences teach us a dear lesson that helps us in the future.

Practice is a part of experience. A piano instructor said that she did not become a pianist until her middle years. She told my wife, "Oh, I took lessons when I was a child.

But taking piano lessons doesn't make you a pianist. *Practice* does!" Practice. Practice. Practice. That is the key to making what you know work for you. Experience produces godliness. (To see what the Scripture has to say about this, look at Rom 5:1-5; 2 Pet 1:4-8.)

And remember one more thing: Practice does not "make perfect." It only makes permanent. What you practice now, right or wrong, will only establish what you will be ten years from now. Experience helps only when we use it to establish right reactions as permanent habits, habits that will build strong walls to keep sin out. Building walls really means renewing the mind.

Activity

The fifth wall is activity. David might never have become involved with Bathsheba if he had been where he belonged —with the army. Activity, being busy with productive work, is a wall against temptation. This is not merely something that we tell little boys—"Stay busy and you'll stay out of trouble." Rather, it is hard, cold fact. Even Geoffrey Chaucer sounds like Solomon when he says, "Idleness is the gate of all harms.—An idle man is like a house that hath no walls; the devils may enter on every side."

Most of us recognize the need to do productive work in order to make our living. We must not be idle in that respect. But in the twentieth-century, Western world, the rush and hurry of life create special pressures. These pressures can often be relieved by doing something for no other reason than that we enjoy doing it. We need to be active in things that bring us satisfaction, since in relieving strain, they help us in our battle against temptation. We need to see more clearly the place recreation has in balancing our lives.

The devil would like to keep us from the things that we enjoy. One of C. S. Lewis's characters, a man in hell reflecting on his earthly life, says: "I see now that I spent most of my life on earth doing *neither* what I ought *nor* what I liked."[4] Lewis continues:

And Nothing [idleness] is very strong: strong enough to steal away a man's best years not in sweet sins but in a dreary flickering of the mind over it knows not what and knows not why, in the gratification of curiosities so feeble that the man is only half aware of them, in drumming of fingers and kicking of heels, in whistling tunes that he does not like, or in the long, dim labyrinth of reveries that have not even lust or ambition to give them relish, but which, once chance association has started them, the creature is too weak and fuddled to shake them off.[5]

Stay interested and busy, not just in things your friends tag "religious," but in the normal, good pursuits of life. After all, they are made holy by the fact that God created them. This kind of life is a gift from God (Eccles 3:11-13; 5:18-20). Activity is a wall to keep sin out.

Common Sense

The sixth wall is common sense. Jesus said, "The children of this world are . . . wiser than the children of light" (Lk 16:8b KJV). An entire book of the Bible—Proverbs—is devoted to short statements about common sense, showing us just how important it is. One Christian leader makes it a regular practice to read a chapter from the book of Proverbs every day.

Often in our search for the "spiritual" answer, we overlook something basic. For example, a young man once prayed, "Lord, what do you want me to do?" The first thought that came to his mind was, "Pick up your socks." He dismissed the thought as silly. Again, on another day, he prayed, "Lord, what do you want me to do?" Again, the first thought that came to his mind was, "Pick up your socks." It was then that the wisdom of the thought struck him, and he realized that the thought qualified as an answer from God. The simple act of regularly and faithfully picking up his clothes is an important step in building a regular, strong, ordered Christian character This *was* what God wanted from him. A simple matter of common sense.

At this moment you may feel, "This book will change my life." But in two years you may even have forgotten that you read it at all, much less retained any valuable points from it.

Strength from the Lord

The seventh wall (and the last I will mention) is strength, help from the Lord. The apostle Paul had faced a continuing affliction that kept reminding him of the fact that he was only a man. To do the work God had given him to do, he was forced to fall back continually on the strength and grace of God. He said, "When I am weak, then I am strong" (2 Cor 12:10b). Remember, "Unless the LORD builds the house, those who build it labor in vain" (Ps 127:1). And unless you labor in the Lord's strength, your wall building is in vain.

For your Bible study you might look prayerfully at 2 Corinthians 1:8-11 and Philippians 4:14 which tell us of our need for strength from the Lord. Other passages tell us how the Lord imparts strength to us (a) by our singleness of purpose (Is 49:4; Jas 1:6-9, (b) in response to prayer (Lk 22:43), (c) in quiet confidence (Is 30:15; Rom 4:20), (d) in quietness (Mt 14:23; Is 30:7, 15; 2 Cor 12:9), (e) in joy (Neh 8:10), (f) in knowledge (Prov 24:5) and (g) in wisdom (Eccles 7:19).

Summary
We should not be surprised to find that self-control does

not come easily. We are complex creatures, and there is much to learn both about the spiritual world and about ourselves.

We can never walk in the Spirit unless we learn self-discipline, an internal system of self-restraint and self-motivation. There is a real sense in which the battle has been won or lost before the temptation ever comes knocking. It is then that we learn whether we have walls or not. If we discover that they are broken down, with the Lord's help, we can rebuild them stone by stone.

The walls that guard against temptation are: understanding, balanced emotions, joy, experience, activity, common sense and the strength of the Lord.

"No temptation has overtaken you that is not common to man. God is faithful, and he will not let you be tempted beyond your strength, but with the temptation will also provide the way of escape" (1 Cor 10:13). Be honest as you think about that verse. It does not say, "the way of *easy* escape." It may be a hard door to walk through, and it may take some doing to find it, for it is not always marked with a brilliantly lighted EXIT sign. But it is there. It is just that finding it and walking through it will take some self-discipline and strong walls.

9

Learn to Run

"Show it a fine pair of heels
and run for it."
Shakespeare (I Henry IV)

"Let us run with perseverence the
race that is set before us."
Hebrews 12:1

ON THE PLAIN OF OLYMPIA, about eighty miles southwest of Corinth, the Greeks held their Olympic games. For five days every four years young men of pure Greek descent gathered and competed. The games were dedicated to the god Zeus.

The contests were so important to the Greeks that the home cities of the winners breeched their own walls to welcome the returning heroes. All wars were suspended at the time of the competition. The prizes included not only fame and great honor, but also a garland of wild olive.

If we can judge Paul's interests by his writings, he must

have been a sports fan. He writes about boxing and running, using these things as pictures of the Christian life. It is possible, perhaps even probable, that Paul attended the Olympic games. His travels took him near the Plain of Olympia, and there would have been perhaps fifteen Olympiads in his lifetime. Whether he witnessed the games or not, he certainly referred to them.

In this last quarter of the twentieth century, running has become a popular activity. I've done some amateur jogging myself and have experienced some of the things to which Paul must have been referring when he compared the Christian life to running. When I began, I was about twenty-nine years old and very much overweight. I'll never forget my first times out. Fifty yards of jogging left me winded and in pain. But for some reason I didn't give up and began a regular program of walking that developed over a period of weeks into jogging.

I can think of at least four illustrations of Christian self-discipline to be found in running: (1) the more we run, the more we are able to run; (2) to run, hindrances must be laid aside; (3) learning to run means learning to endure pain; and (4) Christians must learn to run away from some things and run toward other things.

The More You Run . . .
The Christian life is a long-term race, not a dash. If it were the act of a moment, even a very difficult moment, it would seem almost easy by comparison to what it actually is. But this race lasts a lifetime.

It can be fatal to try to run two miles the first time out. But week by week, from a walk to a run, the speed and distance increase. Muscles become stronger, lungs increase in capacity, blood vessels are scrubbed clean, new blood pathways to the muscles are created, and the heart learns to work hard once again. It is unbelievably satisfying to see it happen and to know that it is happening to you.

In the Christian life, the more and better we live for Christ, the better able we are to live for him. We see parts of the old self fall away and learn to conquer problems that we had once believed could never be conquered. Paul said: "I press on to make it my own, because Christ Jesus has made me his own. . . . Forgetting what lies behind and straining forward to what lies ahead, I press on toward the goal for the prize of the upward call of God in Christ Jesus" (Phil 3:12-14).

Hindrances Laid Aside

Alexander Solzhenitsyn said in *The Gulag Archipelago:*

> If only there were evil people somewhere insidiously committing evil deeds, and it were necessary only to separate them from the rest of us and destroy them. But the line dividing good and evil cuts through the heart of every human being. And who is willing to destroy a piece of his own heart?[1]

Everyone knows that runners strip down to the lightest dress possible. In fact, in Paul's day, the Olympic participants competed with no clothing at all. The writer of Hebrews says that we are to "lay aside every weight" (Heb 12:1). This is a severe act of self-discipline, because the weights that Christians lay aside are not clothes, but actually parts of themselves! The besetting sin has become "me," in that I cannot imagine my life without it. To lay it aside would be to give up a part of my identity.

As Solzhenitsyn points out, the line that divides good and evil does not conveniently run somewhere over to my left, but directly *through me*. Trappers know about the sprung trap that is empty, and the snow drenched with blood about it. Rather than be caught, the animal has chewed off its own leg. This calls to mind Jesus' command: "If your right eye causes you to sin, pluck it out and throw it away. . . .

And if your right hand causes you to sin, cut it off and throw it away; it is better that you lose one of your members than that your whole body go into hell" (Mt 5:29-30).

The difficulty lies, of course, in the pain we experience in laying aside these weights. This brings us to the most important points in this chapter.

Learning to Endure Pain

Looking back, I realize that jogging was an exercise in ignoring aching lungs, side stitch, sore muscles, a raw egg in the back from a passing car, folks pointing fingers and calling out clever remarks, tired legs and the pain of sheer exhaustion. The runner who continues to run learns to simply ignore these things. Thinking about them makes them overwhelming and the novice runner may quit. It is either ignore them or fail.

Paul Hauck has said: "If you cave in on your goals every time you . . . are experiencing discomfort, I guarantee that you . . . will never be well-disciplined. Good self-discipline and suffering go hand in hand."[2] The philosopher John Locke used even sharper words: "He that knows not how to resist the importunity of present pleasure or pain, for the sake of what reason tells him is fit to be done . . . is in danger of never being good for anything."

Today, right and left, we find people giving up because they are having some pain. They give up marriage, jobs, children, school and even life. The frequent, supreme question is, "How do I remove the cause of the pain?" rather than, "How do I learn to endure it?" It isn't wrong to ask that pain be removed and to do what we can to remove it, within limits. But comfort must be secondary to doing whatever must be done to accomplish our goal.

We must face this fact: it is going to be painful to pass up our favorite sin when temptation comes. I have sometimes wondered how it was that I chose to ignore the pain and continued to run. At least part of the answer is that my mind had been so thoroughly persuaded that this *had* to be done that there seemed no other choice. My body said, "Don't!" My mind said, "Run!" Yes, it was painful, but the anticipation of future pleasure decisively outweighed the pain of the present moment. What pleasure was I looking for? A new feeling of vigor. New mental alertness. Clothes that fit. Freedom from the guilt of being lazy and undisciplined. The respect of other people. So when my feet and legs, burning lungs and stinging eyes all said, "Stop this stupidity," all that I knew to be true said, "Keep it up! Ignore those messages from your body!" As in running, so in spiritual growth: learn to ignore the pain, and you will have taken a quantum leap forward in your ability to resist the devil.

Learning to Run Away
There are some temptations that can be dealt with only with your heels. Wellington is quoted as saying, "The best general is one who knows how to conduct a retreat." The great devotional writer of half a century ago, A. J. Gordon, said, "Avoiding temptation is next in importance to resisting temptation." When Jesus gave instruction in prayer, he said that we should pray, "Lead us not into temptation" (Mt 6:13a). And when remonstrating with the sleepy ones in the garden, he urged, "Watch and pray that you may not enter into temptation" (Mt 26:41).

There is an unmistakable message in life and Scripture: "Avoid temptation when you can. Don't walk foolishly into it. Arrange your affairs if possible so that you may avoid it." Of course we don't have total control of our circumstances, but we do have options now and then. The proper option is to "flee also youthful lusts" (2 Tim 2:22), "flee immorality" (1 Cor 6:18), and "flee from idolatry" (1 Cor 10:14b, all KJV).

A river-boat captain was once approached by a man running illegal goods on the river. The man offered the captain a sum of money if he would take his boat to the shore to pick up a load of contraband. The captain refused. The offer was doubled. The captain then drew his pistol, leveled it at the man's head and said, "Every man has his price, and you're getting too close to mine. Now get off this boat!" Truth is, in the area of our own special weakness, most of us have a price which if offered would be almost overwhelming. If you cannot successfully resist, then run.

G. E. Rees said, "Temptation in the line of duty God has provided for; but for temptation sought and coveted, God has made no provision." Surely it is with this thought that Paul tells us, "make no provision for the flesh, to gratify its desires" (Rom 13:14b).

If your weakness is to drink, then you should stay away from those people who would tempt you to it. If being alone in a far-away city opens you up to temptation, do all in your power not to make that trip without a good and reliable friend. If your weakness is drugs, then by every means available to you, stay away from the crowd that uses them. Proverbs 4:14-15 says, "Do not *enter* the path of the wicked, and do not walk in the way of evil men. *Avoid it;* do not go on it."

Running is not all negative. After speaking to Timothy about the love of money, Paul says, "Flee these things" (KJV), but immediately tells him what to run *for;* "righteousness, godliness, faith, love, steadfastness, gentleness. Fight the good fight of the faith; take hold of the eternal life" (1 Tim 6:11-12).

Our prize is not a garland of wild olive leaves, but a crown that does not fade away. This goal kept Paul moving. Yet there is more. In the Roman games, the emperor's private box was positioned immediately overlooking the finish line. As they approached the end of the course, the runners looked to the emperor, for it was from him that the reward was received.

Jesus is the "emperor" of the race of life. He sits at the finish line, and we are told that as we run we are to look to him (Heb 12:2). It is from him that we will receive our "well done," and the crown that will never fade away.

Remembering the Reasons

James Fixx is one of the better-known runners of the 1970s. He has written a popular book, *The Complete Book of Running*. In chapter seven, "Getting Good At It," Fixx says:

> When we race, strange things happen to our minds. The stress of fatigue sometimes makes us forget why we wanted to race in the first place. In one of my early marathons *I found myself unable to think of a single reason for continuing*. Physically and mentally exhausted, I dropped out of the race. Now I won't enter a marathon unless I truly want to finish it. If during the race I can't remember why I wanted to run in it, I tell myself, "Maybe I can't remember now, but I know I had a good reason when I started." I've finally learned how to fight back when my brain starts using tricky arguments.[3]

Christians must also learn to fight back when the tricky arguments come, from whatever source. When faced with temptation, try hard to remember why you decided to follow Christ and why you decided that you must not do the thing that now tempts you.

For example, suppose that your marriage is a miserable mess, but you have decided to be faithful to your marriage commitment. But now, months later, the pain begins to get to you. You feel you have had all you can take of being looked down upon, complained at and nagged. How good it would be just to be free from it all! Try to remember why you decided to keep it all together. Your reasons might include: Jesus placed great importance on the marriage bond; real biblical love means making decisions that are in my partner's best interests and in the best interests of the family and the name of Christ; leaving marriage would make me vulnerable and lonely, perhaps in old age I would be without anyone; my children need the stable influence of parents committed to each other's welfare, even if the fires of affection burn low, and I love my children very much; it is possible that by working hard at the responsible choice, affection can return and the marriage can be warm again; to give up would be a concession to my own weakness, and no spiritual growth would result from that concession; somewhere down the road, the trial would need to be repeated in some other way.

Under the great pressure and pain, you may have difficulty remembering the reasons for your decision. Think, "I can't remember now, but I know that they are good reasons." Talk to someone, a stable, noncritical friend who can keep secrets and can help you remember. This is just one possible example of many kinds of temptations and the reasons for resisting them.

Summary

The long-distance run is still a good illustration of the Christian life. At least four things can be learned about self-discipline from the runner: (1) the more we run, the more we are able to run; (2) hindrances must be laid aside; (3) self-discipline includes learning to endure pain; (4) we must learn to run away.

We are running toward a great prize, Jesus the Author and Finisher of our faith, and a crown that is incorruptible.

10

Accept Chastening

"God sends us many love tokens, and
among them are the great and little
annoyances and pains that beset our lives,
and on each of them, if we would look,
we should see written, in His own hand,
this inscription: 'For your own good.' "
Alexander MacLaren

"For the Lord disciplines him whom
he loves, and chastises every son
whom he receives."
Hebrews 12:6

ALL GOD'S CHILDREN GOT TROUBLE—so the old saying
goes, and so it is. This chapter is about trouble used by God
as a disciplinary tool. It is also about an attitude that allows
the tool to have its intended effect in producing strength,
maturity and holy character.

God chastens his children. The epigraph from Hebrews
12 tells us about it. The passage goes on to say that if God
does not chasten us, we are not true children, but illegitimate imposters (12:8). It is safe to conclude that the difficulties of life "are used by God to shape and polish the
believer as a living stone for the temple of God. Adversity,

prosperity, sickness, disappointment, bereavement, failure and success are tools in the hands of the divine Architect."[1]

Suffering—A Part of Chastening

Someone once told me that when God disciplines, the discipline is painless. The Bible says exactly the opposite. "*All* discipline seems painful rather than pleasant" (Heb 12:11). The psalmist understood this. "The Lord has chastened me sorely, but he has not given me over to death" (Ps 118:18).

There have been occasions when most of us have fallen to our knees and cried out, O God, why did this have to happen? You could so easily have prevented it! How can you be so cruel? Again the psalmist knows: "Thou hast taken me up and thrown me away" (Ps 102:10).

There have been times for me when all seemed lost, and I cried out in deep bitterness, "Why did you not simply cause the circumstances to be different? You could have worked a miracle at any one of a dozen different points and the entire picture would have been changed. We would not have had this pain! Your name would have been honored. The world would have looked on and said, 'See what a wonderful thing God has done for them!'"

How logical! What a tempting line of reasoning! Yet the miserable circumstances prevailed in spite of prayer to the contrary. The loss was sustained. There was nothing to do but, "like a mule in a hail storm, hunker down and take it!"

There are three kinds of situations in which God may discipline a Christian. First, he may send or allow chastening when his child is involved in wrongdoing. The Christian who has become rebellious and unyielding is sure to face a disciplinary measure from God sooner or later. Jeremiah expresses a proper response to this kind of discipline: "I have heard Ephraim bemoaning, 'Thou has chastened me, and I was chastened, like an untrained calf; bring me back

that I may be restored, for thou art the LORD my God' "
(Jer 31:18).

Second, discipline is sent when the Christian needs to
grow in strength, faith, understanding, love or devotion.
James says, "Count it all joy, my brethren, when you meet
various trials, for you know that the testing of your faith
produces steadfastness" (1:2-3). Hardship and testing can
produce results not obtainable otherwise.

A man once found the cocoon of an Emperor moth and
kept it with the purpose of watching the beautiful creature
emerge. Finally the day came and it began to struggle
through the small opening at one end of the cocoon. The
struggle continued for hours, but the moth could never
force its body beyond a certain point.

Finally, believing that something was wrong and that the
opening should have been larger, the man took a pair of
scissors and carefully clipped the restraining threads. The
moth emerged easily, and crawled out onto the window sill.
Its body was large and swollen, its wings small and shriveled. He supposed that in a few hours the wings would
develop into the beautiful objects that he had expected.
But it did not happen. The moth that should have been
a thing of great beauty free to float and fly, spent its short
life dragging around the swollen body and shriveled wings.

The constricting threads and the struggle necessary to
pass through the tiny opening had been God's method of
forcing the fluids from the body into the wings. The "mer-
ciful" snip of the threads was the most cruel thing possible.

Often God lets us struggle rather than stepping in like
a big brother to do our fighting for us. No doubt he could
make it all so easy and every moment of life so pleasant. But
as we struggle, becoming exhausted almost beyond endurance, changes occur in us which could not happen otherwise: the "fluids" expand our wings, and in time we can fly.
Cut the struggle short at some crucial point and we are

crippled forever ... or until God gives another opportunity for struggle that will do what the first aborted struggle should have been allowed to do.

The third set of conditions under which God sends some disciplinary measure is when we need to be restrained in some way. Paul's "thorn" is an example of this. Paul says that his thorn in the flesh was a messenger of Satan sent from God to buffet him and keep him from exalting himself (2 Cor 12:7b). That affliction reached Paul and remained with him in order to restrain him from becoming proud of the unusual amount of grace given to him.

How Can Suffering Help?

God's disciplinary action bears directly on us in the same way that a spanking or a hand of restraint bears upon a child. This is exactly the comparison made in Hebrews 12.

Sometimes our suffering is the direct result of disobedience. We committed a sin and the natural consequence of the sin was pain. Sometimes sin will lead us into circumstances so disgusting and difficult that we come to loathe the sin itself. For example, suppose that you have a secret sin and someone discovers it. You are deeply embarrassed. An obsession with material things can lead to financial disaster; or pride, to social ruin. If we are self-centered, we may lose the respect of our friends. We have all seen cases in which drug use has led to unhappiness, cigarette smoking to illness and death, a home has been destroyed by sexual dalliance, or health impaired by overeating. The list could go on.

When these things happen to us, we learn in two ways: intellectually and emotionally. The pain carries the message deep into our emotional center and results in built-in restraint in the future.

In the past it has been easy for me to make an occasional cutting remark that caused pain to someone. As I look back and see the discomfort that I have caused in that way, pain comes to me. At this moment I can be in instant suffering just by recalling how I hurt someone close to me fifteen or twenty years ago. The memory fills me with sadness and helps me control my tongue today. As a result, it seems to me that my speech has improved to the point of gentleness. If that is true, then this is an area in which through discipline the Lord has helped me toward a true renewing of my mind.

"I'm making you go without supper for your own good." This may sound familiar: parents often say it, and children usually don't believe it. But the writer of Hebrews said that God disciplines us for our own good, *that we may share his holiness* (Heb 12:11).

One difference between God and parents is that parents make mistakes and God does not. He does not lay a single inappropriate burden upon us, but only exactly what it takes to accomplish our good. Paul said, "we are chastened *so that* we may not be condemned along with the world" (1 Cor 11:32). These chastenings are intended to push us away from sin and to press us to him. "Before I was afflicted I went astray, but now I keep thy word. . . . It is *good for me* that I was afflicted, that I might learn thy statutes" (Ps 119:67, 71). We must always remember that the greatest good in the Christian life is not freedom from pain: rather the greatest good is to be like Jesus.

God also uses difficulty to get our attention. When Absalom asked Joab to come and talk with him, Joab ignored him until Absalom set Joab's field of barley on fire. Joab went to see him right away (2 Sam 14). There may be times when we begin to feel that God is an unwarranted interruption in our living, and so we begin to ignore him. We may then suddenly find our barley fields on fire. The method is extremely effective.

You Have a Choice

We cannot choose to escape all chastening, though we wish we could. You probably respond to pain as C. S. Lewis did: You would like to know how I behave when I am experiencing pain, not writing books about it. You need not guess, for I will tell you; I am a great coward. . . . When I think of pain . . . of dull aches that blacken our whole landscape or sudden nauseating pains that knock a man's heart out at one blow. . . . If I knew any way of escape I would crawl through sewers to find it. But what is the good of telling you about my feelings? You know them already: they are the same as yours. I am not arguing that pain is not painful. Pain hurts. That is what the word means. I am only trying to show that the old Christian doctrine of being made "perfect through suffering" is not incredible. To prove it palatable is beyond my design.[2]

So what are our options? Here is where our basic attitude comes in. In the long run, it is our attitude toward God and toward being chastened that will determine what the outcome of our own chastening will be. If we push against it, refuse to accept it, or try to find another way, it will do us no good at all. It is possible for us to continue to rebel, hardening ourselves and allowing all rebellion to remain intact. *It is possible to choose to learn nothing from God's discipline.*

God said, "In vain I have smitten your children; they took no correction" (Jer 2:30). Caleb Colten, an eighteenth-century English churchman, spoke the truth when he said, "the same furnace that liquefied the gold, hardens the clay." You see, it is not that pain and suffering have any value of themselves. They do not. It is the way we humans respond to them that has value or lack of value. Pain is simply a lance used to open a boil in order to allow it to heal. But when the patient struggles, the lance only makes new wounds.

A proper and fruitful response to God's discipline would include understanding that all events in the Christian life are allowed for a purpose (Rom 8:28). This does not stop the arrow from striking, but it does "wipe the poison from the tip." We should take difficult events seriously, asking God what they are intended to do for us (Heb 12:5) or what lesson we should learn.

We should also accept the discipline (Prov 3:11) and endure its difficulties (Heb 12:7). And throughout the discipline, we should be in subjection to God (Heb 12:9) letting the discipline do its work (Jas 1:4). F. F. Bruce said:

> The man who accepts discipline at the hand of God as something designed by his heavenly Father for his good will ceases to feel resentful and rebellious; he has "stilled and quieted" his soul, which thus provides fertile soil for the cultivation of a righteous life, responsive to the will of God.[3]

There is strength and encouragement in knowing that God is at work in this way. Paul and Barnabus went to Lystra, Iconium and Antioch, "*strengthening* the souls of the disciples, exhorting them to continue in the faith, and saying that through many tribulations we must enter the kingdom of God" (Acts 14:22). One of Jesus' final words to the churches was, "Those whom I love, I reprove and chasten" (Rev. 3:19).

Summary

God disciplines his true children to halt rebellion and disobedience, to strengthen, and to restrain from sin. Such suffering helps us overcome temptation because it leads us to abhor the sins that brought the pain.

When discipline comes, we can choose to learn or not to learn from it. If we choose not to learn, only harm results. If we choose to learn, we must: (1) understand that God has allowed the pain for a purpose; (2) take the disci-

pline seriously; (3) accept it; (4) endure it; (5) subject ourselves to God; and (6) let the discipline do its work. Its
work is to build godly character.

11

Build Your
Faith

"To believe is to be strong."
Frederick W. Robertson

"And what more shall I say? For time
would fail me to tell of Gideon, Barak,
Samson, Jephthah, of David and Samuel
and the prophets—who through
faith . . . won strength out of weakness."
Hebrews 11:32, 34

IN LEWIS CARROLL'S *Through the Looking Glass,* the Queen
tells Alice:
   "Now I'll give you something to believe. I'm a hundred
   and one, five months and a day."
   "I can't believe that," said Alice.
   "Can't you?" the Queen said in a pitying tone. "Try
   again; draw a long breath, and shut your eyes."
   Alice laughed. "There's no use trying," she said.
   "One can't believe impossible things."
   "I dare say you haven't had much practice," said the
   Queen. "When I was your age, I always did it for

half an hour a day. Why, sometimes I've believed as many as six impossible things before breakfast."

Dr. Howard Hendricks of Dallas Theological Seminary quoted this dialog, and then said, "Ladies and gentlemen, the unregenerate man on Main Street, U.S.A. is convinced that is the meaning of faith! Take a long breath; close your eyes to facts, to reality, and believe."[1]

I would like to add to Hendrick's observation. It seems to me that Christians, regenerate men and women, also think this is the meaning of faith. If I am right, this is a special tragedy. The Bible tells us that we become Christians by faith (Eph 2:8), we live and grow by faith (Rom 1:17), and we cannot so much as please God without possessing and exercising faith (Heb 11:6). Yet there is the saddening possibility that many Christians do not even know what it is, how it is acquired or how it can grow.

And because faith is an indispensable ingredient for meeting temptation successfully, lack of understanding at this point is perilous. Hebrews 11:24-25 tells us that by faith Moses was able to resist the pleasures of Egypt. 1 John 5:4 says, "and this is the victory that overcomes the world, our faith." Paul used the picture of both the breastplate (1 Thess 5:8) and the shield (Eph 6:16) to illustrate faith's importance. Abraham's obedience was a product of faith (Heb 11:8). "The righteous shall live by faith" is the only statement appearing in the Bible four distinct times (Hab 2:4; Rom 1:17; Gal 3:11; and Heb 10:38).

Please underline in your mind these two things: Without faith you cannot please God, and strong faith produces strong Christians. If faith is understood properly, we are more likely to recognize it when God gives it, and we are more likely to grow in faith. I want to look first at some common mistakes about faith, then at what biblical faith *is*, how it grows and what I can do to help it grow.

Some Common Misconceptions

The first misconception is that faith is belief in something for which there is no evidence. This is the mistake that Hendricks was dealing with when he told the story of Alice and the Queen.

Many evangelical Christians come fearfully close to agreeing with the definition given by the British agnostic Bertrand Russell. Russell wrote, "We may define 'faith' as a firm belief in something for which there is no evidence."[2] Many Christians would be right at home with that statement if we were to add words to make it read like this: "We may define 'faith' as a firm belief in something for which there is no evidence, but which one feels intuitively to be true." This is tragic.

The danger of defining faith in this way is that it leaves the believer at the mercy of every idea that comes down the pike. Whatever appeals to "intuition" becomes persuasive. A friend said to me one day, "Faith is being able to believe anything you are told." Untrue. That is not the definition of *faith*, but of two other words: *credulity* and *gullibility.*

A second misunderstanding occurs when faith and reason are opposed to each other. If one believes this, then reason, which is a gift of God, is not allowed to do what God intended, and faith can never become mature. Faith is built on the best reasons for believing the Bible to be true.

Misconception number three is that faith is the object of faith. Let me explain. Some think that if one has "faith" (that is, for the sake of our illustration, a certain feeling, some energy generated in the mind, a disposition to believe anything) *in* faith, the desired end will occur. Faith (not God) will somehow of itself produce the object sought. This is not what the Bible means by *faith.*

This leads to misunderstanding number four, that faith is a feeling. Suppose a friend of ours prays for the healing

of an aunt, and says to us, "I believe that God is going to heal
Aunt Tessy!"

"Why do you believe that?" we ask.

"I just feel it! There's a warmth, a fullness in my chest, a
presence, a joy!"

Why does he believe it? Because of the way he feels. His
faith is real (there are all kinds of real faith; faith in tossing
salt over your shoulder, or in never seating thirteen at a
table, are one kind), but the *basis* of his faith is a feeling, and
therefore insufficient and unbiblical.

On with the story: Aunt Tess recovers and, as we should,
we thank God. But our friend makes a mental note: remembering how he felt before his aunt recovered, he con-
cludes, perhaps unconsciously, "Now the next time I pray,
if I can feel that way again, the answer is sure to come." So
an error is born; faith becomes feeling, and our friend
spends the rest of his life trying to replicate that "feeling
of faith." What's worse, if he is successful in replicating it,
he calls it "growing in faith."

There is another danger in this error. When we define
believe as "feel," we conclude that faith rises and falls. This
is the logical conclusion if we think faith is feeling, because
all normal feelings fluctuate. A friend described to me an
incident, and then said, "My faith just went like this," and
she made a motion with her hand similar to the downward
lunge of a roller coaster.

What happened to my friend? Did she stop believing that
God exists or that he works in human life, that Jesus re-
deems us, that the Bible is true, or that God will help her
through difficulty? No. She still believed all of that. What
did happen, then? What took the roller-coaster plunge? It
was her feeling. Her faith was still intact, but she did not
know that, and it was a deep concern to her.

True faith will not rise and fall with the tide. It has a
steady quality. A feeling of weakness under a heavy load is

not a lack of faith, but just that, a feeling. This is a good thing to remember: faith may be very strong when emotions are very low.

The fifth misconception is that I need a daily miracle to build my faith. Faith is based on the reliable witness of the Scriptures to the resurrection of Jesus. Supernatural alterations of my circumstances are not necessary for my faith to be strong. In fact, true faith holds steady when it seems that nothing is going well.

It is also a mistake to think that faith must avoid certain questions and facts. Many Christians are afraid of science, thinking that it will uncover something that will disprove the Bible. Both the natural world and the Bible have the same Author. Therefore, all truth is God's truth. Christian faith need not fear valid scientific discoveries.

A few more things faith is not. Faith is not hope. Hope is based on what we want for ourselves; faith is based on what we have good reason to believe God wants for us. Faith is not a tool with which we force God to act. This is what makes Christianity different from magic. Magic is the use of some means to force an act in the spiritual world, and the magician is in control. Faith leaves God in control. As someone has pointed out, any spirit that you can use is not the Spirit of God. Finally, faith is not a leap in the dark, but an intelligent choice based on the revealed will of God.

What Is Biblical Faith?

Scripture does not offer a concise definition of faith in any single verse, though Hebrews 11:1 comes close. Here is a simple composite of the Bible's definitions: "reliance on God and his truth as revealed in the Bible." This covers the full range of faith in all its Christian applications.

Faith has two aspects: conviction and action. Conviction is a matter of the intellect. Certain facts are set before us, and if they seem to adequately support a point, we accept that point as true. Paul gave this account of his faith:

For I am *persuaded*, that neither death, nor life, nor angels, nor principalities, nor powers, nor things present, nor things to come, nor height, nor depth, nor any other creature, shall be able to separate us from the love of God, which is in Christ Jesus our Lord. (Rom 8:38-39 KJV, italics added)

Before Paul became a Christian, he was devoted to the God of Scripture. Why did he believe in this God? In part he believed because of the material universe he saw around him. Without doubt he had sung Psalm 19 which speaks of the heavens as the work of God's hands. In his letter to Rome he makes it clear that the physical universe is evidence of God's existence and attributes (Rom 1:20). Further, he believed because of God's wonderful self-revelation to Israel. Paul accepted the testimony of the fathers (Ps 44:1) and of the Scriptures as factual history.

But why was he convinced that God had made a new covenant with man through Jesus of Nazareth? Had he seen evidence for the validity of this message in the testimony Stephen gave as he died? Probably. He also had a personal encounter with Jesus Christ that must have been wonderfully persuasive. But back of these facts stood the most important ones of all: the life that Jesus of Nazareth lived, his works, and his bodily resurrection. In Jesus he saw the Scriptures fulfilled (Acts 18:28). Through these things the Holy Spirit changed the direction of Paul's thinking and drew Paul to himself.

Faith is also action. You know of course that purely intellectual faith is not adequate. To become *living* faith, it must be acted upon. This involves more than we know perhaps, but certainly includes intellect, emotions, the overcoming of inertia and so on. One must put into action what he or she knows to be true. This is why we used the word *reliance* in our definition. Reliance implies action.

Search the Scriptures and you will find that four characteristics of faith are very important: *quality, placement, quantity* and *source*. Let's look at these four, one by one.

Faith's qualities. Biblical faith has at least four qualities: genuineness, soundness, stability and strength. When Paul wrote to Timothy he expressed confidence in Timothy's *genuine* faith (2 Tim 1:5). By this he meant that Timothy's confidence in God was not faked. In his letter to Titus, Paul spoke of *soundness* of faith (Tit 1:13; 2:2). Soundness deals with faith's structure. It is to be well based, well reasoned, unflawed, healthy, whole, active. To the Colossians he wrote of *stable* faith (Col 2:5). Stability means, of course, that it has a steady, unwavering quality, not moving about from one thing to another. To the church at Rome he wrote of *strong* faith (Rom 4:20). Strong faith is faith that is able to bear the weight that is placed upon it.

Faith's placement. Faith can be of good quality and yet be placed in the wrong thing. There is a certain faith which we are to have in ourselves, another in our automobile tires, and another in the person who prepares our food, and so on. But ultimately faith centers in God himself. We are wrong to place that ultimate confidence in anything or anyone but him. Therefore our faith can be misplaced.

Luke tells us of the storm on the Sea of Galilee, and quotes Jesus as asking the disciples, "Where is your faith?" (Lk 8:25). He did not ask in this case, "How is it that you have no faith?" but "In what have you placed the faith that you do have?" Jesus told us that we are not only to have faith, but that it is to be faith *in God* (Mk 11:22).

Faith's quantity. The Scripture speaks of faith in terms of amount and size: *no* faith (Mk 4:40), *little* faith (Mt 6:30; 8:26; 14:31; 16:8; and Lk 12:28), *growing* faith (Mt 17:20; Lk 17:5-6; 2 Cor 10:15; and 2 Thess 1:3), *great* faith (Mt 8:10; 15:28; Lk 7:9), *all* faith (1 Cor 13:2), and *fullness* of faith (Acts 6:5, 8; 11:24).

Faith's source. Faith comes as a gift from God (Eph 2:8), is given by means of Scripture (Rom 10:17), the work of the Holy Spirit (1 Cor 2:14), and through nature (Rom 1:20; Ps 19). Faith is subject to growth (2 Cor 10:15; 2 Thess 1:3). These passages imply that faith is both gift and stewardship.

How Can We Grow in Faith?

Full-grown faith is not a feeling that has increased in intensity. It is a trust that is genuine, sound, stable, strong and correctly placed which has penetrated into every area of life. Knowing that this is what mature faith is, we can begin to take steps that will help us reach it. Here are some suggestions for producing this growth.

First, apply the faith you now have. As a believer, faith is already a part of your life. You are persuaded of certain things about the Lord's reality, his love for you, about his providing a way of escape from judgment, his ability to work in the details of your life, and about the fact that nothing can come between you and his love. Now act on those confidences. For example, since you believe that God is able to work in the details of your life, pray regularly that he will. Be alert to the answers when they come. As you exercise your existing faith in this and other ways, it will become a steady way of life.

Second, pray about your faith. It is a gift of God, so request more of that gift. In answer, he may permit new problems on which the old faith can work and therefore grow; but in spite of this risk, we are obliged to ask. Pray that your faith will not fail when it is tested. Jesus prayed in this way for Peter (Lk 22:32).

Third, study the Scripture. "Faith cometh by hearing, and hearing by the word of God" (Rom 10:17 KJV). While it is true that other things can strengthen faith, the Scripture is God's primary tool for making it stronger. Every day the Bible's persuasive power should be turned loose on the believer's mind.

Fourth, practice faith in tandem with other biblical virtues. Confidence (faith) has no value as a thing alone. The Scripture speaks of "steadfastness and faith" (2 Thess 1:4), "righteousness, godliness, faith, love, steadfastness, gentleness" (1 Tim 6:11) and so on. Faith is an exercise in futility when practiced apart from the daily duties of life. It literally has no meaning unless applied in behavior (Jas 2:18).

Fifth, study Jesus Christ. It is impossible to examine him too closely. The more careful your investigation, the more amazing you will find him to be and the stronger your faith will become. Remember, when Thomas had questions, Jesus did not say to him, "Shame on you, Thomas." Rather he said in essence, "Examine me and see" (Jn 20:27), and then he presented to Thomas the same evidence that had produced faith in the other disciples.

The Measure of Faith's Growth

The measure of whether your faith has grown—say at the end of a year or a decade—is not: "Have I worked a miracle or had a vision?" The true measure is uncovered by questions such as these: Is my confidence in God harder to shake now than it was? Does my faith go deeper into my emotional life, helping me face crises with greater steadiness? Am I more secure in what I believe? Do I rest in a greater confidence that he will never turn his back on me? Am I "whistling in the dark" when I say that I believe—faking faith—when down inside I have some real reservations and doubts? Have I been studying the Scriptures regularly, with the help of trained and faithful men or women? Am I applying what I believe to the details of my life more often, more automatically? Is prayer an indispensable part of my life? Do I take an active interest in the sick and needy, and in others who hurt? Am I gaining substantial freedom from the old sins? If the answers are positive, then your faith must surely be growing.

The Rest of Faith

I have said much about our efforts to promote the growth of faith and to fight temptation. But the fourth chapter of Hebrews speaks about rest for the people of God, a ceasing from our own works. It seems paradoxical to speak of *laboring* to enter that *rest* (4:11). But C. S. Lewis has resolved the conflict for me by saying that we rest because we are "trying in a less worried way."[3] That describes my experience very well. Now that I understand that he will not turn his back on me, my efforts to live for him are no longer frantic. A failure is not ultimate disaster. I really do "try in a less worried way." The worry is taken out and we work and rest at the same moment.

Faith makes the difference in meeting temptation. Moses turned his back on the pleasures of Egypt because he was absolutely convinced that God was offering him an incomparably greater reward. He could not *see* the reward, but God said that it was there. His choice was made because he had confidence in what God said (Heb 11:25). His confidence (faith) determined his choice when he was faced by temptation. Faith serves *us* in the same way.

Summary

Faith is absolutely necessary if we are to overcome temptation. There are several misunderstandings about faith which can hinder progress: (1) that faith is belief in something for which there is no evidence; (2) that faith and reason are opposed; (3) that faith is the object of faith; (4) that faith is a feeling, or that a feeling is evidence of faith; (5) that faith needs miracles to build it; and (6) that faith must avoid hard questions.

Biblical faith is reliance on God and on his revelation. It comes through persuasion of the intellect. Saving faith comes as we are moved by God to act on the conviction that Christ can be our personal Savior.

Faith has quality, placement and quantity. Its qualities are genuineness, soundness, stability, and strength. Its proper placement is in God. Faith can remain small or grow. Applying the faith we have to our daily living, praying for increased faith, studying Scripture, practicing faith and studying the person of Jesus Christ are all activities which contribute to the growth of faith.

We may measure our growth in faith periodically. As faith becomes stronger, the old life will increasingly fade as our minds are renewed.

12

Focus on the Source of Power

"Faith needs her daily bread."
Dinah Craik

"Keep watching and praying, that you
may not enter into temptation."
Jesus (Mt 26:41 NASB)

IN THE VAST, UNLIMITED EXPANSE and emptiness of deep space floats a collection of stars—a cluster flat, disklike, with arms spiraling out and revolving about their center. There are one hundred billion stars in the cluster, and distances so vast that light itself cannot cross from one edge of the cluster to the other in less than 80,000 years.

Thirty thousand light-years from its center, far out in one of its spiral arms, moving around the center of the cluster at a speed of 134 miles each second, completing a circuit once in two hundred million years, is a medium-sized star. In its heart, atomic fusion transforms its hydrogen into helium, making it glow with a heat of 20,000 degrees in its upper chromosphere. Violent storms leap away from its surface, 360,000 miles into surrounding space.

Trapped by its awesome gravity, spheres of solid matter rotate about the star. They are tiny in comparison to their captor; their total mass is only 1/745 of the star's great mass.

One of those balls, eight light-minutes from the star's fiery face, spinning about its own axis at a thousand miles an hour, hurtling around the star at eighteen and one half miles a second, is different from the others. It is different for it carries on its surface a thing called "life," a characteristic shared by hundreds of different forms that exist in the ball's clear fluids called "water" and "air."

The living things expand, and some move about. The force of their material life comes from the burning star. If the star were to explode they would be blown into an atomic mist. If it were to grow dim and go out, all their force would be lost and they would quickly "die."

Among these living forms is a thing which not only lives but is *aware* that it lives. This awareness of itself is at once its agony and its glory, for because of it, it is also aware of a thing called "pain" and of another called "joy." It knows also that if in some way it should ever be cut off from the great star it would also die, and unlike all the other forms of life, it wants desperately *never* to die.

It does die, though, through the decay of its own internal systems. But it has the ability to produce others of its own kind before dying. These in turn produce others and, after a time, they die too.

This description of our place in the universe sets things in perspective. We need to be reminded of where and what we are, since most of the time we are much too close to ourselves to think clearly about the larger picture.

Beyond serving as a reminder, this description is also an illustration of one of the most basic facts of Christian existence: that as physical life cannot exist without the sun, neither can spiritual life thrive without God. Shut off from the sun's gravitational field this ball would shoot out of orbit and plunge aimlessly through galactic emptiness. Shut away from its light we would be in darkness and die. Held within its gravitational embrace, the earth moves with purpose, balance and order. Open to its light, we have life, health, vision and warmth.

God, who created all the galaxies by his word, and in whom all of our physical life resides (Acts 17:28), is also the Sun of spiritual life. Held in his gravitational field our lives have order and balance. Open to his infinite personality through Jesus Christ, we have life, spiritual health, vision and warmth.

Spiritual Collectors

On a hillside high in the Pyrenees Mountains of France, stands one of the world's first solar furnaces. It is composed of a wall of 9,500 mirrors, each mirror focused on a single point. The wall stands with its back to the sun, and on the opposite hillside, facing the sun and the wall, are scattered 63 large mirrors that track the sun and transfer its rays to the large reflecting wall. In this way the energy of the sun is concentrated to 7,000° F., which can burn quickly through a sheet of solid steel.

In a way similar to the sun, God has power, power for life and for facing the spiritual battle. And in a way similar to the great solar furnace in the Pyrenees, Christians must collect that power and change it into useful energy.

Receiving the strength for living is not done in some esoteric, mystical way, but in a way that every Christian can understand. In the terms of our illustration we could say that we "aim our collectors" toward God. That is, we concentrate our minds on the living Word of God and on God himself through prayer, Bible study and worship. Isaiah said, "They who wait for the LORD shall renew their strength, they shall mount up with wings like eagles, they shall run and not be weary, they shall walk and not faint (Is 40:31).

The sun is a finite source with a limited life span. It will burn out. But God is everlasting (Is 40:28-29). He is our source of strength as long as this battle lasts and beyond. Our devotional life, on which the collecting of that strength depends, consists of at least four basic things: Scripture reading and study, prayer, worship, and service. These four things are foundational in the divine method for the renewing of our minds. You will notice that these collectors of God's strength overlap with ways of causing faith to grow (chapter eleven). This is deliberate, and quite natural.

Scripture is God's primary means for our continual cleansing. Jesus prayed for us: "Sanctify them in the truth; thy word is truth" (Jn 17:17); and he said, "If you continue in my word, you are truly my disciples, and you will know the truth, and the truth will make you free" (Jn 8:31-32). To the Colossians Paul wrote, "Let the word of Christ dwell in you richly" (Col 3:16); and to Timothy: "Till I come, attend to the public reading of scripture" (1 Tim 4:13).

At this point it would be easy to lapse into an unbiblical mysticism by thinking that there is some magical way in which our lives will change just by a daily reading of the Bible. But we must act out what Scripture teaches. Remember James's words about this very thing:

If any one is a hearer of the word and not a doer, he is like a man who observes his natural face in a mirror; for he observes himself and goes away and at once forgets what he was like. But he who looks into the perfect law, the law of liberty, and *perseveres,* being no hearer that forgets but a doer that acts, he shall be blessed in his doing. (Jas 1:23-25, italics added)

But the fact remains that we cannot do what Scripture says

and it cannot cleanse our behavior and renew our minds unless we read and study it. Every Christian has a basic need for a regular, systematic reading of the Holy Scriptures. This is one of the chief disciplines of the Christian life. And there are hundreds of books on Bible study and devotional life to assist us.[1]

Prayer

Reading Scripture is one half of personal communion with the Father. Prayer is the other half. The most significant thing in Moses' life was that "the Lord used to speak to Moses face to face, as a man speaks to his friend" (Ex 33:11). No more profound thing was ever said of Abraham than that he was called "the friend of God" (Jas 2:23). Even now we are told that Jesus is the friend of those who obey him (Jn 15:13-15). The deepest word about prayer is not the word *request,* but the word *friendship.* If we are to be friends of God, prayer is an indispensable part of that relationship.

Prayer has many parts, each in some way important to our vitality. It is joy and sorrow, a battlefield and a place of peace, a pleasure and an agony, laughter and weeping, listening and speaking, requesting and giving, asking and thanking, work and rest. Under different circumstances and at different times it is all of these and more. We cannot determine what it will be on any given day, but we are responsible to pray always (Eph 6:18). It is either pray or faint (Lk 18:1).

Public Worship

One Saturday afternoon I watched the telecast of the world's light-weight boxing championship match. The boxers were a thirty-one-year-old Scotsman and a man from the United States who was six years younger. The Scot was the reigning champion, and the bout was being fought before a crowd of twenty thousand in Glasgow, Scotland. The champion had said before the match that he would rather die than be beaten before his own people; but the younger contender had never before been beaten in a professional contest.

Soon after the match began it became clear that the battle would be close. As I sat watching, I heard something unlike anything I had ever heard before. It was faint at first, but it seemed to be singing—singing at a boxing match! Gradually, it became louder; hundreds and hundreds of male voices singing a strange Scottish melody. I could hardly believe it. They were singing encouragement for their champion. As he fought for his crown, but even more for the respect of the Scottish people, they sang to encourage him.

I have not thought about that contest since without a lump rising in my throat; nor have I thought of it without thinking how like the Christian's battle it was, and how like the role of the church to sing encouragement for its members.

In my eyes the Scotsman was a champion most of all because he would rather have died than be beaten before his own people. And his countrymen stood with him in his most crucial battle. For that, they have my love.

Likewise, in our battles with the powers of darkness, we need each other. Think of how disconcerting it must have been to the challenger to hear the champion's countrymen sing through round after round of that fight. Oh, how the church needs to address itself to this very thing; to encourage each other in the thick of the fight. And, in a way, that is what public worship is.

There is no substitute for gathering with other Christians for prayer, study, worship and hearing the Word of God. It is an act of consummate selfishness and foolishness to say, "I will be a Christian alone, without the church." But sadly, it is said often. Imperfect as it is, the church is one of the most important of God's means for giving us strength to fight the battle. To gather with others in a place where the Scripture is read and preached, where prayer is offered and where opportunity is given to serve, is as vital as private devotions.

Service

Inflow without outflow equals stagnation. One of the strongest themes of the Old Testament prophets was judgment upon a people who enjoyed the blessing of God, but did nothing to lift the burdens of others. Inside and outside the protective walls of our churches and homes are millions who bear the image of our Father, and who are in desperate need of help. Some are believers, but most are not.

Because we are often satisfied with the emotional uplift of a worship service, we feel little drive to serve in the most practical ways of taking a meal to a lonely person, providing transportation to a doctor's appointment, being a friend to a delinquent, or some other act of kindness.

Whatever the reason for our failure to serve, every Christian needs some consistent outlet for service. We are not to be isolationists, no matter how comfortable that may be. Paul said to the Galatians, "As we have opportunity, let us do good to all . . . and especially to those who are of the household of faith" (Gal 6:10).

You may wonder what this has to do with the business of gaining strength for the battle with temptation. Perhaps I can illustrate. George Truett who was for many years pastor of the First Baptist Church in Dallas, Texas, told of a young businessman who came to know Christ and then became a faithful worker in his service. About a year after the young man's conversion, he began to drift and was seen less and less in the church. Then one day he knocked on Dr. Truett's study door. He opened up to his pastor, confessed doubt that he was a Christian at all and asked that his name be removed from the church records.

Wise pastor that he was, Dr. Truett agreed, but asked the young man to come back later in the day to discuss the details of having his name removed. He also asked that in the meantime the young fellow do him a favor, "Take my Bible, or yours, and go across the city to the room of old Mr. Williams and read the Bible to him."

"What? Read the Bible after what I have said to you?"

"Certainly."

At the appointed time the young man returned, laughing as he burst through the door, saying, "Don't say a word to anybody about having my name taken from the church roll—not a word." And he told of going to the old man's room, reading and praying with him, and of rediscovering the joy of his own salvation in the process.

Truett ended the story by saying, "You see the lesson: Get busy! Keep busy for Jesus!"[2]

There is another story told by Lucian, the Greek author and satirist, about Archimedes and the defense of his home city, Syracuse, in Sicily. Archimedes was a mathematician and inventor. During the Roman invasion of Syracuse, a seacoast city, in 212 B.C., Archimedes devoted himself to producing inventions that might repel the invaders. Lucian says that Archimedes had large concave mirrors made, and that men standing on the shore holding the huge mirrors used them to set fire to the sails of the invading ships.

The story may or may not be true; but this is fact: a Christian with his "collectors" set on the "sun" of his life, has a powerful source for his defense against the enemy of our souls.

Summary

God is the Source of strength for our battle, but to appropriate that energy we must focus on him in special ways: Bible study, prayer, corporate worship and service. Together these things will provide us with more than adequate strength for the battles.

13

Know the Purpose of Temptation

"Temptation is the fire that brings
up the scum of the heart."
Thomas Boston

"The fining pot is for silver, and
the furnace for gold; but the LORD trieth
the hearts."
Solomon (Prov 17:3 KJV)

IF WE BELIEVE THAT WE ARE doing useless work, our
energies are drained away by resentment. But if we understand its purpose, we can attack the problems of the task
at hand with devotion and strength. For the same reason, it
makes a substantial difference in our ability to deal with
temptation if we know what its purposes are.

On the surface, temptation seems pointless. More than
that, it seems impossible that a holy God could allow them.
Some have suggested that God and Satan are equal in
power and are fighting a stand-off battle. Sometimes, so
they say, it seems that God is winning and other times,

Satan. Oliver Wendell Holmes wrote a limerick that expresses the idea.

God's plan made a hopeful beginning,
But man spoiled his chances by sinning.
 We trust that the story
 Will end in God's glory;
But, at present, the other side's winning.

Fun to read; but is it true? No. God has infinite strength, while Satan is a limited creature.

Someone else has suggested that God does not know what the devil is doing at a given time or what he will do in the future, and so is unable to stop him. But this idea is laid to rest by Isaiah: "I am God, and there is none like me, declaring the end from the beginning . . ." (46:9-10). Clearly, God knows all that the enemy will do.

God Permits Temptation

A council was held in heaven, and in the council Satan stood before God. God's question to the Dark Earth Invader was designed to teach something to Satan and to all other created angelic beings. "Have you thought about my servant Job?" Yes, Satan had thought about Job. He knew that Job was blameless and upright before God, but Satan hurled a challenge that constituted something of a demand. He wanted God to allow him to put Job to the test, and God said, "Go ahead."

Suffering came on Job thick and fast, and this brought severe temptation. Job was tempted to distrust his own salvation (Job 4:7), to turn his back on God (2:9), and even to end his own life by suicide (2:9). He yielded to none of these temptations, and as a result a point was proved in heaven.

We have another example with Peter. Jesus revealed that another council had been held in heaven, and this time Peter was the object of discussion. Jesus said to Peter,

"Simon, Simon, behold, Satan demanded to have you, that he might sift you like wheat, but I have prayed for you that your faith may not fail; and when you have turned again, strengthen your brethren" (Lk 22:31-32). G. Campbell Morgan translates, "Satan has obtained you by asking," and then adds, "That is the real force of the Greek verb. It is not merely that Satan had asked; he had obtained him by asking."[1]

From these two passages we learn that Satan is on a leash; he can go so far, but no farther. He cannot tempt or bring suffering without God's direct permission. Morgan put the picture in unforgettable words, "He [Satan] cannot touch a hair on the back of a camel that Job owns, until he has God's permission to do it."[2] This is comforting, stabilizing knowledge. I am not at the mercy of Satan's caprice, but in the guarded care of my Father.

The Divine Demonstration Project
We are thrown back to the initial question, "Why does God allow temptation?" He allows it because of what I call the divine demonstration project. Paul says that God is allowing the great drama of life to unfold in order "that through the church the manifold wisdom of God might now be made known to the principalities and powers in the heavenly places" (Eph 3:10). E. K. Simpson said of this passage:

A galaxy of higher intelligences . . . mark the unfolding of her [the church's] destiny. The church is a spectacle to angels as well as men. From her chequered story and long-drawn conflict the celestial hosts *learn secrets of the Creator's wisdom* not elsewhere divulged. The strange vicissitudes in her status, the yet stranger throes of tribulation through which she is called to pass . . . are *fraught with priceless instruction to these sons of the morning. . . . We are their graduating school.*[3]

Shakespeare said more than he knew, or more than we

take him to mean, when he said:

All the world's a stage,
And all the men and women merely players.
They have their exits and their entrances;
And one man in his time plays many parts.

As You Like It, Act II, Sc. 7

Seated in the theater are the created beings of the unseen worlds: angels of the rank and file, and angels of great authority such as Michael and Gabriel. The Dark Prince himself is there (Job 1:7; 2:2; 1 Pet 5:8), along with the evil ones who were with him in his fall. Unknown to us, our actions, responses, words and deeds are being witnessed at this moment by spiritual beings. When the play is over and the last curtain falls, "every knee [shall] bow, in heaven and on earth and under the earth, and every tongue confess that Jesus Christ is Lord, to the glory of God the Father" (Phil 2:10-11).

We are assured then, that life's temptations are a part of God's demonstration to watching spiritual beings. I have a life to live and a full set of life situations to encounter. If I live it rightly and faithfully, not only will the angelic beings learn something new, but there will be rejoicing among the holy angels. If I fail, something of God's character will be learned in spite of my failure, but I will supply no cause for rejoicing, unless it should be to the keen eye of the fallen ones.

I must add this. We are not pawns on a board. Pawns are mindless things with no will of their own. We have minds and we have wills, and we frame our own responses, either in complicity with evil or in cooperation with our Father.

Other Benefits

There are, of course, side benefits for us. We gain strength if we meet the challenge successfully:

We rejoice in our sufferings, knowing that suffering produces endurance, and endurance produces character, and character produces hope, and hope does not disappoint us, because God's love has been poured into our hearts through the Holy Spirit which has been given to us. (Rom 5:3-5)

Count it all joy, my brethren, when you meet various trials, for you know that the testing of your faith produces steadfastness. And let steadfastness have its full effect, that you may be perfect and complete, lacking in nothing. (Jas 1:2-4)

And obviously there is a refining process going on. As Thomas Boston said, "Temptation is the fire that brings up the scum of the heart." When the scum appears, the great Refiner skims it off, and the molten gold is one step closer to purity.

You might interpret what we have said here to mean that there are no losers in the end. That would be a misunderstanding. There is loss, and there are losers. Because of the Fall, everyone, *including God,* suffers and loses something. There are those who will ultimately lose everything and to whom no eternal good will come. Because God loves these eternal losers, he also knows pain and loss.

Summary
Our attitude toward the battle and our performance as soldiers will improve when we understand why temptation must be a part of life. Ephesians 3:10 reveals that the events in our lives are allowed as a demonstration to teach things about God. This means that our temptations accomplish something—far more than we had ever dreamed. We will face trials with a lighter spirit when we realize day by day that the hammer of temptation never falls without purpose and that our Father has measured the force of each blow.

14

Temptation and Psychological Problems

"The diseases of the mind are more
numerous and more destructive
than those of the body."
Cicero

"A double-minded man [is] unstable
in all his ways."
James (1:7-8)

"APART FROM THE SACRIFICIAL figure on the cross and
the blessed emptiness of the tomb, at present God is showing his love for me most in the office of a Christian clinical
psychologist."[1] That was written by Joan Jacobs, a Christian
wife and mother from the state of California.

The purpose of this chapter is to point out that psychological problems are real, that Christians have them,
that they weaken the individual's ability to be effective
against temptation, and that help for these problems can be
found.

It's All in Your Head

Someone may have said that very thing to you. "It's all in your head." It may be true, but even if it is true, the problem is no less real. Mental blocks and illnesses are genuine and affect life in absolutely concrete ways. Someone has joked, "It's an issue of mind over matter—if you don't mind, it doesn't matter." But there's the rub. We do mind, and it does matter. It matters to God; it matters to the Christian, and because it has a direct bearing on our behavior, it matters to all society.

Mental problems are not only real, but they affect more people than we usually think. In chapter one I illustrated the prevalence of mental problems by saying that out of any twenty-five children in a school yard, only eight or ten would be fairly normal, the rest would have some degree of psychological problem. So you see, we are not just talking about the alcoholic or the person locked up in an institution, but about people you know. We may even be talking about you; the chances that we are is something more than fifty-fifty.

Christians are not immune to mental disturbance. Their brains work just as do those of non-Christians; their experiences hit them just as hard; and their misunderstandings promote psychological twistings in the same way.

God does not suspend natural law for us. Gravity is gravity; electricity is electricity; a malfunctioning gland is a malfunctioning gland, and a psychological trauma a psychological trauma. A bad family pattern is exactly that, and confused thought patterns are the same whether one is a believer or not. The normal consequences of each of these flow into the Christian's life just as they do into the life of the non-Christian. God does not place a fence around the Christian's brain or personality and say, "These shall never malfunction nor become confused."

What Are Mental Problems?

By *mental problems* I mean any condition of the thinking process, conscious or unconscious, that cripples the ability to make proper adjustments to life. There are many different kinds of such conditions, and they make themselves known in varied degrees and have various causes. A profound mental illness that prevents one from functioning in society is called a psychosis. A less profound disturbance is called a neurosis. As a general rule, the things one does as a result of these conditions are different from normal behavior not in kind, but in amount, intensity and in the inappropriate ways they are applied to life.

The causes of psychological disturbance vary. They may be due to poor upbringing, the way we have dealt with our own upbringing, the choices we have made, our methods of coping with problems, something we were taught, a traumatic event, pressures that were too great for us, thought patterns into which we have fallen, actual physical abnormalities of the brain or of the glands that influence the brain, some genetically determined predispositions (toward depression, for example), and even our environment. (For example, a single exposure to some pesticides such as dieldrin, malathion and parathion can alter one's brain activity as shown on EEG's for a full year, bringing loss of memory, loss of sexual drive, difficulty in concentration and irritable behavior.[2] The presence of some chemicals in our foods can produce hyperactivity in children.[3]) All of these are factors in personal balance.

It is now also clear that significant personality changes sometimes occur as a result of small, undetected strokes that may begin as early as one's thirties. Certain other medical problems (for example, hypoglycemia) have a bearing on our disposition and therefore on our ability to get along with others.

Good psychological integration makes it easier to behave

in the right way. Poor psychological integration makes it more difficult. C. S. Lewis speaks of three imaginary men called to war. All three were afraid, but the first man had soundness of mind necessary to deal with his fear, and so acted bravely. The other two were in a psychological condition that prevented them from overcoming their fears. Both of these men were helped by psychotherapy and then were able to make a free choice about their participation in the war. Lewis says, "Well, it is just then that the psychological problem is over and the moral problem begins." One of the men chose to serve his country, and the other to act in total selfishness. Lewis adds:

When a man who has been perverted from his youth and taught that cruelty is the right thing, does some tiny little kindness, or refrains from some cruelty he might have committed . . . he may, in God's eyes, be doing more than you and I would do if we gave up life itself for a friend.

It would seem as well to put this the other way round. Some of us who seem quite nice people may, in fact, have made so little use of good heredity and a good upbringing that we are really worse than those whom we regard as fiends. Can we be quite certain how we should have behaved if we had been saddled with the psychological outfit, and then with the bad upbringing, and then with the power, say, of Himmler? That is why Christians are told not to judge. We see only the results which a man's choices make out of his raw material. But God does not judge him on the raw material at all, but on what he has done with it. Most of man's psychological make-up is probably due to his body: when his body dies all that will fall off him, and the real central man, the thing that chose, that made the best or the worst out of this material, will stand naked. All sorts of nice things which we thought our own, but which were really due to a good digestion, will fall off some of us: all sorts of nasty things which were due to complexes or bad health will fall off others. We shall then, for the first time, see every one as he really was. There will be surprises.[4]

A Warning

All this is not to excuse bad behavior. No excuses. But there are often hidden causes. There is no way around it: mental problems place some limit on freedom of choice. Some Christians will say that environment, the past and the psychological and physical equipment have no bearing on behavior; that all of us are totally free to do right all of the time. The secular determinist says exactly the opposite— that no one is free to choose at any time. The position of the Bible and the best science lies somewhere between the two: that no choices are completely free because no one is perfect psychologically, nor unrestricted by physical or historical conditions.

But the problem lies just here. No mortal knows the degree of freedom (and therefore responsibility) that another has, and no mortal knows perfectly his or her *own* degree of responsibility. This implies that each person is responsible to do all that is possible with the equipment he or she has, by the grace of God, to behave Christianly. Of course someone will say, "You are wrong! Remember Philippians 4:13, "I can do all things in him who strengthens me." Yes, you can: all those things which God sees that you ought to do, considering your equipment and his grace.

The evil person will use what I have said to excuse wrong behavior. On the other hand, the sincere Christian who heartily desires to live a righteous life will *not* take this chapter as an excuse. To that person it will be an encouragement to seek and find help from the proper quarter, and then to go on and live a more effective and a more Christlike life.

Please understand that in most cases of psychological

abnormality, the psychological factors only *predispose* the person to act in certain ways. *Predispose* is not the same as *force*. We are spiritual beings and in most cases the spiritual part of us has enough input to influence our decisions to some degree. The choice may be very hard to implement because it is made against the grain of our psychological and physiological make-up. Drs. Frank Minirth and Paul Meier, practicing Christian psychiatrists have said, "As physicians who have researched genetics quite thoroughly, we get disgusted with people who blame everything on their 'bad genes'!"[5] We must learn what our predispositions are, and then learn to fight courageously against those which are undesirable.

Should Christians Seek Psychological Help?

For some people—including some Christians—there is a time when it is appropriate and necessary to seek psychological help in the fight against temptation and mental problems. Some of the most fervent Christians I know are also some of the most neurotic. It even seems that the way they apply the Bible to their lives brings out the worst of their neuroses.

Some people think that the whole idea of psychology is contrary to the idea of finding spiritual solutions to our problems. Those who think that need to examine their use of the word *spiritual*. Remember, David killed Goliath under the anointing of God. It was a spiritual act. Yet, the stone which David used was a very earthly, material object. If it were to be picked up and examined, nothing special would be noticed about it. It was an object of spiritual use because it was in the hand of a youth who relied on God for its effectiveness. Good psychology is like that stone. In the hands of a skilled practitioner who relies on God for its effectiveness, it becomes a thing of spiritual strength.

When our physical body is sick, our first step is to pray

and seek the best medical help. Our mental problems should be handled in the same way. As increased knowledge in medicine is a gift of increased dominion over creation which the twentieth-century Christian can enjoy and use, so increased knowledge in psychology is a similar gift for the Christian's help and enjoyment. Confronted with a psychological need which hinders obedience to God, the Christian has an obligation to find help.

How Do I Know That I Need Help?

In the context of the problem of temptation, several things indicate that some kind of psychological counseling is in order.

First, when any problem of sin does not yield to prayer, Bible study, discipline and the normal means of grace, help should be sought. By *yield,* I mean that it increasingly comes under the control of the believer's will.

Second, when the unyielding problem contributes to disruption of work, inner peace, relationships or home life, there is special reason for finding help. For example, if you find that you are hypercritical, complaining, angry and in general making life hard for those about you and are unable to bring the condition under control, then everyone suffers and it is your obligation to take action.

Third, when life has a disintegrating quality, something is significantly wrong. For example, a man in his mid-twenties asked an older Christian to advise him about the disorder and confusion he was beginning to experience. The youth told the man that he could not attain consistency in his devotional life, in spite of the fact that he had tried very hard to do so. In addition, he could not attain consistency in his work habits. His social life was also suffering. More and more he was retreating into his own shell.

The friend advised him, "If it were just a matter of regularity in your devotions I would say that you have a spiritual problem—something that has come between you and God —that must be settled. But since you have the same problem in every part of your life, I would say that you have a psychological disturbance and should find a psychologist to help you." Immediately the friend followed through by putting the young man in touch with a competent psychologist. The youth learned that he was becoming disoriented because of depression. He did indeed need help, and the help gave him a whole new start in life.

Fourth, immediate help should be found when one cannot control actions which are illegal or that offer special threat to other individuals, home or society. Some examples of this kind of thing are violent anger, uncontrolled sexual behavior (exhibitionism, child molestation, rape), kleptomania, child abuse, compulsive lying, and so on. Such behavior must be stopped immediately.

Several years ago I worked with a young man in trouble with the juvenile court. He was sixteen and had been caught burglarizing a home. He had been burglarizing homes for some time, but had never taken anything but the underclothing of teen-age girls. He had accumulated enough to fill a large trash bag. He knew the dangers, but until he was caught and ordered to receive professional help, he could not deal with the urge to do it. I sometimes drove him to his counseling appointments, and he was so ashamed of what he had done, that whenever we met another car on the road he would pull his coat collar over his face.

This young man's problem was powered by a drive that had become twisted and had grown beyond his power to control. These disproportionate drives have immense emotional content and power. Of course the person is not driven by the desire continually, and at times may actually feel that it has been beaten and will never return. This "victory" may be interpreted as an answer to prayer. But the problem usually comes out of hiding again, and finds the person just as weak in its presence as before. All the reasons for not doing the thing lose their persuasiveness and are burned up like dry grass before a wind-driven prairie fire.

Of course not all problems are as exotic as this young burglar's. There are many less obvious ones. All of us know people who are driven in a similar way by alcohol, and a good many more who have the same problem with food. But whatever it is, it is a symptom. Of course it is sin too. But the point here is that it is symptomatic of a deeper problem, one that requires special help. Prayer alone will not do the job. One of the characteristics of such a problem is that the more you pray about it, the more you concentrate on breaking its hold, the tighter its grip becomes.

It is this fact that leads me to believe that the legalistic church is especially dangerous to good mental health and right living. Concentrating so heavily on what one "must not do," creates a neurosis in which these very things become twisted drives that control its less balanced members. A pastor friend who was serving a congregation with a very legalistic past told me with amazement of the bizarre kinds of problems that his people were having in their private lives. I asked him outright, "Do you believe that the church's legalism actually *produced* those abnormalities in the people?"

He answered, "I'm convinced of it!" How strange it is, and how characteristic of this fallen world, that our very desire to do right, pursued with intense desperation, may actually make doing wrong more likely.

Once again, when any problem of sin does not yield to the normal disciplines and the normal means of grace, help should be sought.

How Do I Choose a Counselor?
Having determined that there is a need, how does a Chris-

tian select a counselor? This is not an easy problem, in spite of the fact that there are many psychologists available. For the Christian there are two distinct questions to answer in making this choice: "Is the counselor a Christian? If not, how will he or she treat my Christian beliefs? Is this counselor competent?"

In 1947, C. S. Lewis wrote to a friend: "Keep clear of psychiatrists unless you know that they are also Christians. Otherwise they start with the assumption that your religion is an illusion and try to 'cure' it." A look at some of the writings of well-known psychiatrists show that Lewis was right—at least about *some* psychiatrists.

But it is extremely important to see that there are many psychologists who respect Christian beliefs, even though they are not themselves Christian. These men and women have many practical insights to give. A non-Christian counselor who has respect for Christians and what they believe can be of great help.

Now the second question, "Is this counselor competent?" Recommendations of other professionals—medical doctors and pastors—whom you trust may be your only guide. But that a doctor, psychologist or counselor is a Christian is no guarantee of competence. It isn't unusual to hear someone say, "Oh, you should go to Dr. So & So. He's a Christian." The truth is that some doctors graduated at the bottom of the class, and some Christians are among them. Some Christian professionals are competent; some are not. Brilliance, skill or the ability to apply knowledge does not always accompany faith in Christ. If I needed a gall bladder removed and were given a choice between a highly skilled, brilliant surgeon who was an avowed atheist and a devout Christian with a reputation as a blunderer, I would take the atheist. My faith can make up for his atheism, but I cannot create skill to compensate for the other's incompetency. By analogy, the same is true for psychologists.

Whatever your circumstances, if you are in need, I urge you to go to whatever lengths are necessary to find a counselor who is both competent and who will respect your Christian experience.

A Serious Matter

Whatever we do, we must learn to take problems seriously, both the problems that we have and those of others. When troubled people come to us we must not treat their problems lightly. Their concern must be taken at face value. It is a devastating experience to search out a friend, reveal your heart, and then to have your friend laugh and say, "Oh, it's not all that bad! You're doing fine!"

We must learn to stop giving pat, simplistic answers to complex human problems. Most troubled people have already tried the short cuts and are looking for answers that will give them a real handle on their trouble.

Cotton Mather, the Puritan theologian, once said, "That which cannot be cured can be endured." True, but none of us would want to return to the day when diphtheria and polio could not be cured, and one could do nothing other than bear the terrible consequences bravely.

It appears to be the will of God for humans to gain a progressively greater dominion over the earth, so that more and more can be cured. That's well for us. We are not like churchmen of the last century who disapproved of the use of the new anesthetics for women in childbirth. They objected on the grounds of Genesis 3:16: "In pain you shall bring forth children," fearing that the will of God would be thwarted by the use of ether.

Psychology is—or can be—part of this increased dominion. We can be grateful for the help psychology gives over mental problems. Of course its power could easily be overstated; it is not a cure-all. Alone, without the grace of God, it is nothing more than a Band-Aid. But as a tool in the hands of a faithful man or woman, it is a positive help. It can be useful for the true transformation of minds (Rom 12:2).

Summary

This chapter, as much as any other in this book, deals with Romans 12, "be transformed by the renewal of your mind." Many Christians have found that psychology has been able to help them over an impassable block in that process. There are danger signs to tell us when we need that extra help.

Joan Jacobs, the housewife and mother whose quotation opened this chapter, said, "I believe many persons in conservative pews could use some straight talk from the satisfied customer of a good . . . psychologist. . . . As the kinks straighten I find my experience with God renewed. I've discovered how much he really loves me. I know him better."[6] That's the whole point!

Part Three

Strictly for
Encouragement

15

You Lost a Battle—
Don't Lose the War

"One does not need to read far in the
Gospels . . . to see the particular
care that Jesus Christ had for the weak."
Paul Tournier

"A righteous man falls seven times,
and rises again."
Solomon (Prov 24:16)

A FRIEND AND I WERE TALKING one day about a lady whom
we both know and to whom we had tried to be a help. Her
story was an especially tragic one. She had married at an
early age, lived a life of poverty and given birth to several
children. An extended period of mental illness overtook
her, and she was placed in a hospital. When finally released,
she found that her children had been taken by the state and
given new homes. Much of the rest of her life was spent
trying to find her family. She was broken in health, alone,
compelled to make her own living and deeply discouraged
with all of life

As I discussed her situation with my friend, I made one of those empty comments one makes when one is not thinking: "I think she feels she's a failure."

He responded, "Maybe she is." Of course he was right. Though it was not her intentional doing, life had been a long string of failures.

Admitting the Facts

We make a mistake if we think that if God is at work in our lives, we will be perfect. When we see that we are not perfect, we are hesitant to admit it, for fear that others will think that we really are not Christians. Besides, we are ashamed.

I am not saying that we should hang our dirty laundry out for all to see. That would be a mistake in the other direction. But we ought to be honest enough that others can see we are not "china saints." It is good for us to admit our imperfections.

As important as anything else I have said—about prayer, Bible study, self-discipline, chastisement, and knowing the enemy's tactics—is this: there will not be a single day in our lives when we do not need the redeeming grace of God in Jesus Christ. From this it follows that *fail* is what all humans do; *continue to try* is what all Christians do; and *accept erring Christians* is what God does.

"Christians are not perfect—just forgiven." So says one bumper sticker that is wiser than most. This is not to say that we make no progress and do not become more like Christ. We do. But can you think of a single person in either the Old or New Testaments, other than Jesus himself, whose life was an unbroken line of growth? I think not. In fact, if we could know in detail the lives of the biblical characters, we would probably see that many of them advanced in the same way we do, by taking three steps forward and two steps back.

Shame

And what is to be my attitude toward myself when I have sinned? When I have taken that step backwards? This is the focal point of this chapter. In spite of confession and forgiveness, we experience a thing called "shame." It is possible to be so overwhelmed by shame that we lose all will to go on.

Shame is not the same as guilt. Rather, shame is regret, true sorrow at knowing that even by the grace of God, we are not good enough to avoid sin. It is a wish to hide. To dwell on shame can drive us wild with hopelessness. Guilt is dissolved at Calvary. But shame? That's something different.

We should recognize that shame itself is a good sign, at least within limits. After enumerating the sins of Jerusalem, God asks, "Were they ashamed when they committed abomination? No, they were not at all ashamed; they did not know how to blush" (Jer 6:15). Shame, then, is an appropriate emotion when we have sinned. But of course, it is not a pleasant experience, and we cannot bear it for long without serious effects. Over twenty years before this writing, while in my late teens, I was acquainted with a man who experienced great shame, discouragement and, finally, God's rescue.

He was in his late fifties and a Christian leader in his rural community. Everyone knew his testimony and knew that he had raised an unusually dedicated Christian family. He was manager of the small local office of a large grain company. But one day it was discovered that there were deficits in grain amounting to many thousands of dollars. It was finally determined that he was responsible for the missing grain, and he stood trial. He was found guilty and sentenced to repay the loss.

His shame was great. He went to work for a rancher, driving a mule-drawn wagon, feeding cattle. In the summers he traveled with custom wheat cutters, following the harvest from Oklahoma in the spring to near the Canadian border in the fall. He dropped from the life of the church and the community, literally hiding his face in shame.

In the autumn of the worst year of his life, the cutting crew was in the Dakotas. One Saturday night the men camped outside of a small South Dakota town. On Sunday morning he rose, dressed and walked into the little town before dawn. Lost in his shame and discouragement he walked to the town's park and sat down on a bench, waiting for the sun to rise.

As he sat there, he made a decision. This would be the day for ending his miserable life. Somehow he would commit suicide. It was the most bitter moment of all his life. But it was in that moment that he glanced up and saw a very old man walking toward him from the east over the top of a hill. He walked out of the sunrise, straight to where my friend was sitting. The old man looked down at him and said only these words, "Young man, God sent me here to tell you that he still loves you!" With that, he turned and walked back over the hill. My friend sat there weeping at the sheer wonder of God's love and the intensely personal way he expressed it that morning at sunrise.

That day marked the beginning of his return to active, public Christian life. He was still ashamed, but no longer overwhelmed, for God had driven home the fact that he cared for him and that he was "accepted in the Beloved." I know of no reason to think that God looks upon you or me in our failure any differently than he did on my friend. Accepting God's acceptance is the only way we can keep the shadowy fingers of the past from dragging us into despair. From there it is our business to accept and have affection for ourselves. This is God's answer to shame.

He Doesn't Walk Away

"Jesus doesn't turn around and walk away when we fail him" one preacher said one Sunday morning. After the service, a rather hard-nosed legalist buttonholed the preacher who had made that statement and told him he was wrong. But that preacher was no. wrong; he was right. And those words were confirmed for me on a very personal level.

I too have lost some battles. The most serious of all came about ten years ago. It was the kind of bitter experience that has repercussions until the last days of earthly life. Not only was it serious, but a substantial share of the fault was mine, and I knew it. If I live to be a hundred, there can never be enough years between the present and that day.

During this crisis, I went with a group of young people on a wilderness survival trip high into the Colorado Rockies. Several days into the expedition, weary from hiking, feeling remorse, confusion, shame and emotional exhaustion because of what I had temporarily left behind, I wandered away from the group to do some thinking and praying alone.

There was no Bible in my pack, so as I gazed down a slope into a turbid river, I was desperately searching my mind for a passage of Scripture that would speak to the confusion and sin inside. Nothing. Absently I reached out my hand to a single dried reed in front of me, took hold of it and snapped it cleanly off. These words flooded my mind. "A bruised reed he will not break, and a dimly burning wick he will not quench" (Is 42:3). I knew that though I was a failure, weak, bruised and with little life or strength left, God would not aggravate my agony, would not destroy me. That lesson has been one of the most important of my life.

God has said, "I will never fail you, nor forsake you" (Heb 13:5). We are as secure as a small child pressed close to the breast of a loving mother. This does not mean that our behavior does not matter; it matters very much. Paul said, "Are we to continue in sin that grace may abound? By no means!" (Rom 6:1-2). But when we do fail, it means that we are not rejected. Given an atmosphere free from the threat of being turned out, a child can grow and mature in calm security. Yes, the child is disciplined, sometimes with severity, but never turned away from family and home.

C. S. Lewis once wrote "to a Lady" some words that may appropriately be repeated here:

> I know all about the despair of overcoming chronic temptations. It is not serious, provided self-offended petulance, annoyance at breaking records, impatience, etc. don't get the upper hand. *No amount* of falls will really undo us if we keep on picking ourselves up each time. We shall be v[ery] muddy and tattered children by the time we reach home. But the bathrooms are all ready, the towels put out, and the clean clothes in the airing cupboard. The only fatal thing is to lose one's temper and give it up. It is when we notice the dirt that God is most present in us; it is the v[ery] sign of his presence.[1]

Summary

Failure will always be a part of life on this earth. When we fail we must admit it, pick ourselves up and begin again. We may experience shame when we fail. Shame is the appropriate feeling of regret for our failure. It should not cripple us, but serve as an indication that our conscience is sensitive to sin.

You may have lost a battle, most likely you have lost a good many. But unless you give up trusting him, you haven't lost the war.

16

When the War Is Over

"I'm gonna lay down my sword and shield,
Down by the riverside.
Ain't gonna study war no more."
A Spiritual

"And they overcame him. . . ."
A Voice in Heaven (Rev 12:11 KJV)

IT MAY BE THAT IN THE LIBRARIES of heaven, there will be a complete history of the human race. If there is, it will no doubt include an account of wars—the campaigns of Alexander, the Gallic Wars, the sack of Rome, the wars of Napoleon, and others. Surely it will contain place names such as Trafalgar, Waterloo, Hastings, Saratoga, and Iwo Jima, and among others the names of Darius, Tamerlane, Charles Martel, Nelson, Simon Bolivar, Asoka, and MacArthur.

But none of those battles, no matter how pivotal, will be the most important in such an account. The battle about which we have written in these pages will hold center stage. After all, the struggle with temptation is the battle out of which all others have grown.

Past Tense

On September 2, 1945, I was only a little boy, and I had no idea of what was taking place on the decks of the great battleship Missouri, at anchor in Tokyo Bay, her decks filled with Americans and Japanese. But I do remember something of the three shadowy years before that day. I remember the nightly voices of Kaltenborn and Beaty, the talk of mysterious places with names like Singapore, Guam and the South China Sea. I remember a threatening atmosphere and even a fear that we might be invaded.

During the storming of Tarawa, the campaigns in North Africa, the Battle of the Coral Sea, and Midway, the end of the war seemed impossibly far away. And for nearly four hundred thousand of our soldiers, the war's end would never come. But for most, the day finally dawned when the battles were done. I remember that day in 1945 when there were smiles everywhere, and the streets were filled with cars, their horns blaring in celebration. The War was over! We had won. It was all in the past.

Because we have always lived with struggle, we find it hard to believe that someday the struggle will all be over. We want to believe it, but we are like children promised some wonderful thing on Christmas morning. They feel that the day will never come when they really will have that bicycle or doll. "School will never be out!" "It will never be time for our trip to the mountains!" On long drives children ask, "When are we going to get there, Daddy?" And when we tell them, they say, "I can't wait!" But of course they do wait, and so shall we.

Our problem is compounded by the fact that we have no one of flesh and blood to whom we can talk who will tell

us, "I've been there!" In the heat of the fight we are likely
to begin to say to ourselves, "Maybe I'm just following a
pipe dream." That's a good time to remember what Albert
Einstein once said, "When you sit with a nice girl for two
hours, you think its only a minute. But when you sit on a hot
stove for a minute, you think it's two hours. That's relativ-
ity." Time is relative: when life becomes uncomfortable
with trial and testing, heaven seems a very long way off.

Yet, Revelation 12 speaks of the conflict entirely as in
the past. "There *was* war.... The great dragon *was* cast
down.... They over*came* him...." God, who sees the future as we see the present, revealed to John a scene from the
"postwar" era. When that day actually comes, we too will
speak of the present in the past tense.

Heaven Will Come
Of course this life here is not all battle, blood and sorrow.
The colors and sounds of the earth are very sweet; we are
pleasantly intoxicated by them. Work is often a joy. Human
relationships bring satisfaction and pleasure beyond words.
There are times when I feel that I never want to leave this
place, no matter how beautiful and good heaven may be.
But on the other hand, when I see more clearly the suffering of the race, especially the little children, then the other
side of the picture comes flooding in upon me. I realize
that we have deep enjoyment only when we are successful
in forgetting that even in our best moments countless
others are suffering immeasurably. When we take off the
blinders, then, all things considered, there are many reasons to long for heaven as Paul did (Phil 1:23).

We know very little about heaven. Often folk think of it
as being a static sort of place where we will float about as
invisible beings, singing, bowing and little else. That is a
mistake. Jesus has a resurrected body in heaven, and Scripture assures us that our resurrected bodies will be like his.

He spoke of places to live; and Revelation 22 tells of a river, trees, light and other similar things. It is certain to be a place of great beauty, thought and activity.

My personal hopes for heaven go beyond even these things. It is not unreasonable to hope that we will meet Christians from all periods of time, and that we can sit down and talk with them, even develop deep friendships. Think of becoming a close friend of someone like Abraham Lincoln or George Washington Carver. Time will not separate you from such people. There you will be the contemporary of every Christian who has ever lived!

Heaven will be a place of continued learning. We can learn from Martin Luther the details of the Reformation; from angelic friends what roles they played in the events of the nations. I have visions of a choir composed of the best voices of all history singing the "Messiah" as Handel himself directs! Can you imagine the "Hallelujah Chorus" as that choir would sing it?

Perhaps you would awake one morning to hear a knock on your door and open it to find Jesus standing there. He might say to you, "Today you and I will walk among the trees down by the river. I'll explain some things to you and answer the questions you have asked all the years before you came here."

And what of your body? Perhaps it has been a very long time since you could run and leap like a child through tall spring grass. Maybe you have never been able to do it. There you will be able. All the marks of aging—aching joints, shortened breath, lost hearing—all of that will be washed away as dust in a spring shower. Life will be new and unspeakably better than ever before.

Think even of broken relationships here, the unapproachable person, the Christian from whom you have been alienated by some misunderstanding or circumstance. There the barriers to affection and perfect relationships will be gone. Your inability to express yourself freely will disappear. All friendships will be mended and the joys of open hearts will flow like a river.

The heartbreak of every child who has suffered here will be healed. Every abused child, every lonely person, all will receive compensatory joy. The marks of physical and psychological abuse, of impatience and hate, poverty and starvation, the twistings of the mind will all be gone under heaven's healing touch.

There we will never be interrupted by a message of death. There will be no funerals, no graveyards, no hospitals. Its shores will never be threatened by invasion. Its homes will be secure and its country lanes safe to walk. We will work with our minds and our hands to produce ideas and things of beauty. As God has desired and created, so shall we. The effaced image will be restored. While the context of 1 Corinthians 2:9 speaks of something other than heaven, surely its words apply to heaven as well. "As it is written, 'What no eye has seen, nor ear heard, nor the heart of man conceived, what God has prepared for those who love him.' "

Welcome Home!

What will it be like to reach heaven? A story out of the recent past may give us some idea. During June, July and August of 1965, an ordinary man from Cleveland, Ohio lived out a dream. Forty-six-year-old Robert Manry purchased a thirteen-and-one-half foot, thirty-year-old, dilapidated boat. He repaired her, christened her "Tinkerbelle" and learned to sail. Then on June 1, 1965, his dream began. He set out from Falmouth, Massachusetts for Falmouth, England, far across the Atlantic.

Manry's voyage was to take seventy-eight days, many of them cold, wet and painful. Hit by storms, confused by hallucinations of hitchhikers and assassins, washed overboard, delayed by winds that were too great and becalmed by lack of any wind at all, plagued by loneliness and troubled by saltwater sores, he kept sailing.

Manry expected to sail into Falmouth Harbor quietly, let his family know of his arrival, secure passage for himself and Tinkerbelle, and return to the States. It did not turn out quite that way. Word of his voyage had reached England. As he neared the coast, Shackleton bombers from the R.A.F.'s forty-second squadron flew over in salute. Newspaper teams from both sides of the Atlantic vied for his story. Great ships hove alongside with congratulatory messages.

During the last miles a flotilla of ships and boats sailed out of Falmouth to greet him. Royal Navy helicopters formed an umbrella above. Boats circled and flocked about him and the people called out, "Good show!" "Glad you made it, mate!" "Well done! Well done!" Sailing along the quay he could see crowds of cheering people jamming the ramparts of Pendennis Castle. Manry later wrote:

People were everywhere; standing along the shore, perched on window ledges, leaning out of doorways, crowded onto jetties, thronging the streets, clinging to trees, and cramming the inner harbor in boats of every size and description. The whole place was teeming with humanity. I heard later that 50,000 people were there to see Tinkerbelle and me complete our voyage.

I was dumbfounded, numbed by the enormity of it all and not a little bewildered. It was just too much to take in all at once . . . every boat and ship in the harbor let go with its horn or whistle and shook the whole waterfront with reverberating sound as the crowd yelled. R.A.F. Shackletons flew overhead in wigwagging salutes and a band . . . St. Stythians Silver Band, played "The Star-Spangled Banner" and "The Stars and Stripes Forever."[1]

Perhaps you think I am being fanciful to say that it will be something like that to reach heaven; but I don't think so. If the angels rejoice at the time of our conversion, what will they do when we finally come home? And what of the others who arrived there before us and have anxiously awaited our coming?

It may not be very long before we anchor there. In the meantime, be absorbed with your life; live with balance; take joy in your work, and you will find that the time will pass soon enough. One day we will sail out of the fog, out of the storm and smoke of battle, out of the choppy sea and into a harbor of calm, blue waters. The wind will hush, and our sails will drop down empty as we glide into a cheering welcome and deep, full life. Swords will be sheathed, cannon and arms stowed. We will see his face and hear his voice saying, "Well done!" The battle will be past. We will have won by the blood of the Lamb. The war will be over!

Notes

Chapter One: The External Problem
[1]C. Everett Koop, *Whatever Happened to the Human Race?* A tape-recorded discussion based on the film series (Los Gatos, Ca.: Franky Schaeffer V Productions, 1979).
[2]B. F. Skinner, *Beyond Freedom and Dignity* (New York: Bantam Books, 1972), p. 190.
[3]Barbara Graustark with Janet Huck, "The Long Hot Summer," *Newsweek* 93, no. 14 (2 April 1979): 59.
[4]Murray Banks, *How to Live with Yourself,* (New York: Murmil Associates, a tape-recorded lecture).
[5]Israel Government Tourist Office, An Advertisement, *National Geographic* 123, no. 5 (May 1963).

Chapter Two: The Internal Problem
[1]Roger A. Caras, *Dangerous to Man* (Philadelphia: Chilton Books, 1964), p. 320.
[2]William F. Arndt and F. Wilbur Gingrich, *A Greek-English Lexicon of the New Testament,* 4th ed. (Chicago: Univ. of Chicago Press, 1952), p. 273.
[3]G. Campbell Morgan, *The Westminster Pulpit,* 10 vols. (Old Tappan, N.J.: Fleming H. Revell, n.d.), 2:69.

Chapter Three: What Causes Weakness?
[1]Morgan, *The Westminster Pulpit,* 9:78.
[2]Francis Schaeffer, *True Spirituality* (Wheaton, Ill.: Tyndale House, 1971), p. 129.

[3]Paul Tournier, *The Strong and the Weak* (Philadelphia: Westminster Press, 1977), p. 204.

[4]Ibid., p. 206.

[5]E. M. Blaiklock, "The Breath of Hell," *Christianity Today* 20, no. 16 (7 May 1976): 13.

[6]D. Elton Trueblood, *The Encourager* (Nashville: Broadman Press, 1978), p. 124.

[7]Alexander MacLaren, *The Life of David* (Grand Rapids: Baker Book House, 1955), p. 4.

[8]Ibid.

[9]C. S. Lewis, "Communicating," *Decision* 16, no. 11 (November 1975): 13.

Chapter Four: Change Your Mind

[1]Gordon R. Taylor, *The Natural History of the Human Mind* (New York: E. P. Dutton, 1979), p. 134.

[2]Lewis Thomas, *The Medusa and the Snail* (New York: Viking Press, 1978).

[3]Clarence Edward MacCartney, ed., *Great Sermons of the World* (Grand Rapids: Baker Book House, 1958), p. 308.

Chapter Five: Know What God Expects

[1]Schaeffer, *True Spirituality,* p. 136.

[2]Craig Ladwig, "The Holdeman: A Nation Apart," *The Kansas City Times,* 26 December 1977, Section A, p. 18.

[3]C. S. Lewis, *Mere Christianity* (New York: Macmillan, 1960), p. 145.

Chapter Six: Know Your Enemy

[1]Lewis, *Mere Christianity,* pp. 123-24.

[2]James Dobson, *Preparing for Adolescence* (Santa Ana, Cal.: Vision House, 1978), pp. 86-87.

[3]Edward Lindemann, "Letters," *Science News* 111, no. 1 (1 January 1977): 3.

Chapter Seven: Walk by the Spirit

[1]John Peter Lange, *Lange's Commentary on the Holy Scriptures,* vol. 9 (Grand Rapids: Zondervan, 1960), p. 31.

[2]Those who wish to study the work of the Holy Spirit more carefully should read John R. W. Stott's *The Baptism and Fullness of the Holy Spirit* (Downers Grove, Ill.: InterVarsity Press, 1964).

Chapter Eight: Build Your Walls

[1]Barbara Spence, "Death of a Marriage," HIS magazine 40, no. 5 (February 1980): 1.

[2]Gordon Taylor, *The Natural History of the Mind* (New York: Dutton,

1979), p. 28.
[3]"Ann Landers," *Garden City Telegram,* n.d.
[4]C. S. Lewis, *The Screwtape Letters* (New York: Macmillan, 1958), p. 64.
[5]Ibid.

Chapter Nine: Learn to Run
[1]Cited in "Points to Ponder," *Reader's Digest,* November 1979, p. 50.
[2]Paul Hauck, *How to Do What You Want to Do* (Philadelphia: Westminster Press, 1976), p. 80.
[3]James Fixx, *The Complete Book of Running* (New York: Random House, 1977), p. 92 (italics added).

Chapter Ten: Accept Chastening
[1]Robert D. Brinsmead, "Sanctification: It's Human Factor," *Present Truth,* special issue, 1975, p. 5.
[2]C. S. Lewis, *The Problem of Pain* (New York: Macmillan, 1962), p. 105.
[3]F. F. Bruce, *The Epistle to the Hebrews* (Grand Rapids: Eerdmans, 1964), p. 361.

Chapter Eleven: Build Your Faith
[1]Howard Hendricks, "What Faith Is," *Moody Monthly* 73, no. 9 (May 1973): 40.
[2]Bertrand Russell, *Human Society in Ethics and Politics* (Edison, N.J.: Allen and Unwin, 1954), p. 215.
[3]Lewis, *Mere Christianity,* p. 129.

Chapter Twelve: Focus on the Source of Power
[1]Books to improve your devotional life:
John Baillie, *A Diary of Private Prayer* (New York: Charles Scribner's Sons, 1949).
Oswald Chambers, *My Utmost for His Highest* (New York: Dodd, Mead & Co., 1935).
Richard J. Foster, *Celebration of Discipline* (New York: Harper and Row, 1978).
Hanna Whitall Smith, *The Christian's Secret of a Happy Life* (Old Tappan, N.J.: Fleming H. Revell, 1942).
Books to improve your Bible study:
John R. W. Stott, *Understanding the Bible* (Grand Rapids, Mich.: Zondervan, 1980).
T. Norton Sterrett, *How to Understand Your Bible* (Downers Grove, Ill.: InterVarsity Press, 1974).
[2]George W. Truett, *A Quest for Souls* (New York: Doran Company, 1917), p. 301.

Chapter Thirteen: Know the Purpose of Temptation
[1]G. Campbell Morgan, *The Gospel According to Luke* (Old Tappan, N.J.: Fleming H. Revell, 1931), p. 247.
[2]Ibid.
[3]E. K. Simpson and F. F. Bruce, *Commentary on the Epistles to the Ephesians and Colossians* (Grand Rapids: Eerdmans, 1957), pp. 75-76, (italics added).

Chapter Fourteen: Temptation and Psychological Problems
[1]Joan L. Jacobs, "The Christian and the Head-Spreader," *Christianity Today* 18, no. 9 (1 February 1974): 4.
[2]Robert Trotter, ed., "Pesticides Can Alter Brain Activity" in *Science News* 114, no. 25 (16 December 1978): 424.
[3]Robert Trotter, ed., "Additives at Fault in Hyperactivity" in *Science News* 117, no. 13 (29 March 1980): 199.
[4]Lewis, *Mere Christianity*, pp. 85-86.
[5]Frank Minirth and Paul Meier, *Happiness Is a Choice* (Grand Rapids: Baker Book House, 1979), p. 43.
[6]Jacobs, p. 4.

Chapter Fifteen: You Lost a Battle—Don't Lose the War
[1]W. H. Lewis, ed., *Letters of C. S. Lewis* (New York: Harcourt Brace Jovanovich, 1966), p. 199.

Chapter Sixteen: When the War Is Over
[1]Robert Manry, *Tinkerbelle* (New York: Harper and Row, 1965-66), pp. 226-27.